Webcast Profit Toolkit:

How to Share Your Message, Engage an Audience and Get More Customers with Your Own Live Interactive Online TV Show

by Mike Koenigs

Table of Contents

FREE BOOK UPDATES AND VIDEO TRAINING

This book is INTERACTIVE - to get a training video about webcasting and how you can use it to start or grow a business, the audiobook version, for free, and/or updates to this book when new versions are released, **visit** www.WebcastProfitToolkit.com

Endorsements

"There are those who lead and those who follow and then there are trend creators. Mike is the latter who uses his creative genius and relentless pursuit of new frontiers and technologies to change the landscape of what is possible and usable in today's crazy, ever-changing business landscape."

John Assaraf,
NY Times Bestselling Author, Founder PraxisNow.com

. . . .

"I feel very blessed to have Mike Koenigs as a friend and in my personal and business life. After many years of teaching people around the world, it is guys like Mike Koenigs that keeps me sharp. And, we both share the same goals of wanting to help millions of entrepreneurs achieve their goals to greater financial and business success. More people need to engage in Mike's teachings – quite amazing!"

Brian Tracy, Author, Speaker, Entrepreneur

. . . .

"There are very few visionaries who can truly look into the future and pluck from thin air the next big thing, not just once, but time after time - Tom Peters, Faith Popcorn, Sean Parker. Mike Koenigs breathes that rarified air. He's done it no less than eleven times over the past 20 years. But, unlike most, Mike not only sees the future, he monetizes it. In each of those twelve cases he took his vision and turned it into a successful million dollar plus business in fewer than 100 days. Whether he is teaching based on actual results (not theory), simplifying complex systems into digestible bites, extracting the genius from interviews with the most interesting people in the world or selling millions in front of the camera, I can think of no one better equipped to share with you the actionable knowledge Mike has distilled into his latest book."

Roland Frasier - CEO, All Channels Media

. . . .

"Building a business or product takes a lot of work and is usually too daunting so most of us fail. But then there is Mike Koenigs. I have never seen anyone else have such a passion and ability to automate, teach and simplify any business process. He helps turn anyone into a superstar business stud. Thanks Mike!"

Eric Berman, CEO of Brandetize

. . . .

"Mike Koenigs and I are in a mastermind group together and I have known him for several years. He is without question one of the smartest marketers I know. He's also one of the most deliberate, studied, systematic, focused and scientific entrepreneurs I know. I would recommend anything Mike produces because it is always top quality and delivers massive value. When it comes to business, he's the guy you want to be when you grow up :)"

Glen Ledwell CEO & Co Founder, Mind Movies LLC

. . . .

"Mike never ceases to amaze me with his ability to to spot and capitalize cutting edge business and marketing trends and then turn around and make it simple for anyone else to do the same. From the tools he creates to the training he provides, Mike knows what it takes to succeed quickly. As a bestselling publisher and consultant myself, I have often found myself asking "What would Mike Do?" Instead of reinventing the wheel, I simply steer it in his direction. Many people achieve success, only a few people can lead others to success as well as Mike Koenigs."

Brad Costanzo, CEO of Costanzo Marketing Group and Host of Bacon Wrapped Business

. . . .

Introduction

Dear Friend,

Welcome to the Webcast Profit Toolkit, my nineth #1 bestselling book.

This represents nearly 25 years of hard work, experience and the efforts of my incredible team and customers. Maybe you're one of them!

I wanted to take a moment to share some thoughts with you in no particular order about what to expect in this book.

First, it's interactive. There are lots of opportunities for you to go deeper in the content, gain access to several free training videos, participate in some interactive webcast events and register to get updates to this book as it gets expanded and I correct the inevitable errors, grammar and spelling mistakes, that are bound to be in here.

In fact, if you find any mistakes, **PLEASE** tell me by sending the error and page you found it on to my email MikeKoenigs@gmail.com. Thanks in advance.

Second, this book is for business. It's intended to help you grow your business, produce qualified leads and make money.

Third, it's for implementers. You'll see there's LOTS of ideas that you can use to grow any business type. If you're the type who's looking for free, easy money, this isn't the book for you. I'm not here to blow smoke up your butt and lie to you.

Fourth, this book wasn't intended to be a NY Times #1 Bestseller. It's designed to give you some actionable strategies you can implement to make great content, shows and video. The secondary purpose is to start a conversation with you, give us a chance to get to know each other better, develop trust, a bond and ultimately help us decide if we will work together someday.

Fifth, this is a book that's packed with content and lots of ideas. It's a WHAT book, not a step-by-step HOW TO book. My intention and the purpose of this book is to show you the most powerful ways to market yourself, expose you to multiple ways to promote yourself with live interactive online video, build a list, gain exposure and leverage the latest technology and strategies available and set yourself up for long-term growth and make your own interactive online show in the future. We have a how-to system available that includes everything you need to execute what you read in these pages.

I'll be the first to admit, I'm a shameless self-promoter - and I want to help you reach more people, make more money and add value to your life and everyone you come in contact with. You'll notice there are opportunities throughout this book to register and watch videos and YES, I do have some great products I'd like to sell to you because they work and you'll have a better life with them.

If you don't like the book, that's ok. I'll refund your $0.99. Just forward your Amazon receipt to my email address and my assistant will take care of you. Please don't leave a negative review because you found a spelling or grammar error. I already had stage 3a colorectal cancer - I know what a _**real**_ pain in the ass is. I'm over it. Life's too short for malcontents, haters, trolls, whiners and complainers, ok? We can part as friends and leave it at that.

Having said that, if you like what you read, or most of what you read, I'd absolutely, positively love to hear from you and get to know you better and find out what you learned - or better yet, post a picture or video on my facebook wall at www.Facebook.com/koenigs and/or Tweet me at @MikeKoenigs.

The BEST way to start a relationship with me will be to visit www.WebcastProfitToolkit.com, watch the free training videos, post your comments on the comment wall and I'll do my best to respond to you.

I'm looking forward to getting to know you better!

Sincerely,
Mike Koenigs in San Diego, California, USA

Foreword

"Here's to the crazy ones. The rebels. The troublemakers. The ones who see things differently. While some may see them as the crazy ones, we see genius. Because the people who are crazy enough to think they can change the world, are the ones who do."

"Think Different" Apple Commercial

I remember it like it was yesterday—the moment I realized I had just made a million dollars *in a week*.

The date was November 17th, 2009. I was in the car when my first-generation iPhone rang (I've always been an early adopter). It was my bookkeeper. He shared some *very good news* with me. We had just launched a product and sold over one million dollars of a program I had created *in a week.*

I smiled, hung up the phone and called my mom.

When she answered, I started to cry.

Uncontrollable sobs. It must have sounded to her like I was hyperventilating.

"Mike?" she asked. "Are you OK? What's wrong honey?" I paused.

"It's not what's wrong, Mom," I said. "It's what's right." I paused to regain my composure and took a couple deep breaths.

"Do remember how I always said I wanted to make a million dollars someday?"

"Oh yes, dear. That's what you wanted to be when you grew up, a millionaire," I could hear her soft smile through the phone.

"Well Mom. I did it. I just made a million dollars...in a week."

But even as I said those words, I knew that it was more like...

Twenty-three years. Plus one week.
That's more accurate.

Twenty-three years of trial, error, and failure and frustration. Twenty-three years of discovery, insight, breakthrough, and success. Twenty-three years to learn how to make a million dollars in a week.

It was like a lottery ticket, but as I told my Mom, "Best of all, I know how to do it again. I've finally cracked the code."

For six more years, I tested, refined, and streamlined the system. And each time I tried, it worked with increasing effectiveness and decreased risk and at one point, generating *$9.1 million dollars in a week*.

I called my Mom that day too. When I told her the news, she said:

"Wow, honey...that's better than a million dollars, isn't it?" Yes. Yes it is.

If you want to learn the system for million dollar days or multi-million dollar weeks, you have two choices. Spend the next twenty-years testing, tweaking, tracking, and trying like I did.

Or read this book.

Inside these pages, I outline my system for making more, giving more, and living more using webcasts - live interactive online shows.

As long as you are willing to stretch yourself a bit, you'll be able to create your own media network, TV channel, and following on your own, without having to rely on producers, publishers, or your cranky assistant (and her bad hair days).

I'll show you how to do this...
...even if you're afraid of being on camera.
...even if you hate technology.
...and even if you don't think you can sell or don't like selling.

This system is yours and I ask for nothing in return other than to implement and have you share your results with me.

The world needs to hear your message...and if you don't share it, who will?

Some Context - My Background

I grew up in Eagle Lake, Minnesota (Population 763).

My dad worked the equivalent of four jobs; he was a barber, the city clerk, the town building inspector and favorite entertainer at the local rest home where he played his guitar and performed for the elderly folks. In his "spare time" he sharpened scissors to make extra money.

My mom was busy raising four children of which I was the oldest. There wasn't a lot of money to go around and I remember, even at a young age, wanting more... I wanted to spend time with my dad. But he was always working. I didn't want my parent's life. I didn't want to live in the harsh, cold Minnesota Winters. I never wanted to hear those words, "we can't afford it." Ever.

I wanted to be rich.

Adults would ask me, "What do you want to be when you grow up?"

My answer was always, "I want to be a millionaire." I would pour over the direct mail letters and catalogs. I always left the JC Penney catalog a shredded mess of dog-eared pages and circled the gadgets and toys I wanted when I had the money... someday. A fantasized about things I'd do or make...if I could afford the tools to make them.

There were lots of problems with my millionaire plan, the first of which was my serious struggle with ADHD. I had the attention span of a bag of gnats on amphetamines. My grades were horrible: "Mike is very... creative..." were the teachers comments on my C- and D+ report cards. I wasn't good at sports: "There's Mike Koenigs in the outfield... ball coming straight for him... will he catch it??!!... Oh, wait, nope... he's throwing his glove at a moth...PAY ATTENTION!" And truthfully, there was little hope of me amounting to much of anything. I couldn't even follow in my father's footsteps—who wanted half a haircut?

Instead, I filled my time with other things; TV, movies, and computers. (Even as I write that, I can hear mothers across the world cringing at the thought of "excessive game-playing screen time,") but for me, it was the most valuable education I'd ever receive. I taught myself to program at age 14, back in 1981 — before most people even knew what a computer was.

I was good at taking things apart. Figuring out how they worked. Figuring out how to make them better. And putting stuff back together...unless I got distracted...

In my teens, I was writing invoicing programs for $10 an hour while my friends were flippin' burgers for $3 an hour. Of course, $10 an hour was still a long way from a million and I had no way to replicate or scale my work, but even then... I had a suspicion I was onto something.

Have you ever had that suspicion...? That maybe there's more to you than meets the eye or can be measured by standard testing?

In addition to programming, there was something else that excited my inner geek (oh who am I kidding, there was nothing "inner" about my geekiness), and that was...

Pitchmen and infomercials.

As I kid I used to love going to the (legendary) Minnesota State Fair to watch the pitchmen. I'd stand in the crowd, munching on a bucket of cheese curds, studying their every move and word. I'd watch as they wrapped up their sales pitch and half the audience would walk up with their wallets open, buying whatever kitchen gadget, garden tool, goop, cleanser or miracle doo-dad they were selling.

At the time, I didn't know what "influence" or "salesmanship" was; I thought the pitchmen had magical powers. And I wanted to know how their tricks worked! Because unlike magicians, who are mostly broke, these guys were making money in minutes. Crowds of people were like living ATM machines, handing out money in exchange for a gadget (and some entertainment). My untrained brain couldn't quite grasp the nuances of their skills and I was desperate to tap into their powers — to get trained, mentored or something.

Then, in the 80's, infomercials became commonplace when the US congress passed a law allowing 30 minute infomercials to be broadcast on TV. One of my very favorite infomercials was for BluBlocker Sunglasses. Do you remember that infomercial? It's the one where Joe Sugarman walked down Venice Beach with a camera and said, "Put these sunglasses on and tell me what you see." And people just went nuts for them with visual social proof of their reactions:

"They're so clear!"

"It's like everything is in 3D!"

One guy even started rapping about the sunglasses. Nevermind the fact that *all* sunglasses show the world in 3D (because the world *is* in 3D), or the fact that the viewer never actually got to put a pair on… simply watching the raw, emotional reaction of others was enough to turn viewers into believers. Joe went on to sell almost a billion dollars' worth of sunglasses with BluBlockers.

20 years later, I still had BluBlockers on my mind—not because I needed sunglasses, but because I wanted to test the power of video and sales. By this time, I was a successful programmer—I taught myself how to put video on a web page long before it was as easy as pushing a button on a smartphone and uploading to YouTube. "Wow," I thought. "If people will buy stuff when they watch a video… what better place to put those videos than online." So I returned to trying to crack the online infomercial code.

After hearing me talk of my fascination with infomercials, a friend made some calls on my behalf and introduced me to some of the earliest infomercial pioneers; people like Tim Hawthorne, Nancy Marcum and a few others who had sold billions of dollars worth of products on TV with infomercials. After overcoming the initial boy-band shock of meeting them, I said to each, "I think I can make the infomercial work online… Can you tell me the secrets behind the television infomercial formula and the power of video persuasion?"

Each agreed to help. They let me interview them. They sent me their scripts. Tim Hawthorne produced a video for me that deconstructed the "classic" television infomercial. Then with a stroke of luck, I was at an event and met Joe "BluBlockers" Sugarman. He gave me his bestselling infomercials to put into my first information product and helped me understand why they worked so well. I called it The Internet Infomercial Toolkit.

I sold the product for $997 to a couple hundred people… It wasn't a million dollars, but it was exciting! And even more exciting? YouTube came out one year later and suddenly I was the online-video guy.

I took the opportunity and ran with it!

First, I built a tool for distributing video and generating traffic - it was called "Traffic Geyser". Then, I created a communication system that allows people to capture leads and build relationships with people online with mobile and social media marketing called "Instant Customer".

We put together a product launch to sell that product online.

It only took 1 week to make a million dollars.
Well, one week, and twenty-three years.

Five months later, I produced another product. This time, we took everything we learned and included my secret weapon in the launch — the online-pitchman-infomercial-masterpiece:

A Live Webcast.

I can still remember glancing down at my computer screen when the first order came in after displaying the "Buy Now" button. It was electrifying. "Yes!" I thought. "It's working!" We kept presenting and the orders kept coming…

And kept coming.
And kept coming.
And kept coming.

That product launch went on to produce $9.1 million in gross revenue—and now get this, $3.1 million of that revenue was made on a single webcast—a live interactive online broadcast... a highly-engaging, entertaining, educational infomercial that viewers could interact with me and my guests in real-time.

For *12 hours* we conducted interviews, gave away valuable content, invited our customers in to tell their transformational stories and pitched our product over, and over again. And while no one "rapped" about our program, I'm certain even Joe Sugarman was impressed.

Since then my companies have produced and generated well over $40 million in launch revenue. I don't tell you that to brag. I tell you that because over half that revenue came from doing webcasts—and a webcast, is something anyone can do with a computer and a webcam.

And webcasts can help you if you:
- Like to help people
- Can answer questions or can ask an expert questions
- Are passionate
- And want to change the quality of your life

Because here's the thing: $20 million in webcast revenue comes at a price. I've made mistakes and felt the fear of massive failure breathing down my neck. However, through those trials have emerged fail-proof answers and learning-shortcuts. After spending nearly 30 years "in the trenches", I've created a formula that *anyone* can use to produce a audience-engaging, revenue-generating *event* that consistently produces results.

I've been many things in my life; I've been poor, I've been the underdog, I've been the geek in the outfield more interested in catching moths or my own thing than the game everyone else was playing. I've made and lost millions of dollars. I'm a son. A father. A husband. Like you, I am and have been many, many things. But there's one thing I've never been...

And that's behind the curve on the next big digital breakthrough in sales, product creation, audience engagement and "intimacy" creation...

Webcasting is the NEXT BIG THING.

And it's yours for the taking because very few people even know what it is or the power it can give you.

But that's what I'm going to teach you in this book.

Since my first live webcast in 2008 I have been teaching this process to others in over 60 countries; across many markets, with varied products and the result is always the same—huge success. (You'll read some of their stories later in this book). The webcasting process is replicable, learnable, and it works. Any business, anywhere in the world, anytime webcasting is the future.

And I don't want you to miss it.

In the following chapters I am going to reveal to you the secrets behind this multi million-dollar model. I will teach you exactly how I, and those I've worked with, have generated enormous amounts of income by connecting with audiences in this live, intimate, and lucrative way.

I believe webcasting is the future of selling with video. The days of infomercials are basically over because the cost of television and media broadcasting are so high. The days of traditional broadcasting as we know it are gone. Social media by itself is already *old fashioned*. There are over 4 billion people online right now (and billions more are expected to be online in the next 24 months). You can literally turn on your phone and broadcast your message and talk to the *planet*...for free...

But what good is contact with the planet if it's a one-way conversation?

With webcasting, unlike with traditional methods, the planet can actually talk back. *You can read the minds of your audience with live interactive chat.*

We live in the single, greatest moment in human history; where you can turn on your computer and chat with 1, 100, 1000, 100,000 people simultaneously. You can create, sell and deliver products, or simply have a real-time conversation. Think about the people you'll reach. The lives you'll change. Yes, the money that comes with being the first to a worldwide trend is nice, but when a comment comes across your live chat that says you saved their life... nothing means more than that.

Not even a million dollars.

When I was a kid, wanting to become a millionaire, there was no way for me to know there would be something better than a million-dollars-earned... But now I understand.

It's never actually about the money...It's about the impact. What matters more than a million dollars is the amount of impact that million creates—an impact felt around the world by dreamers just like you and me who want to make a difference and make things that matter. It's that learned skill of looking around the world and seeing opportunity everywhere - and being able to turn that vision into a reality.

Don't get me wrong - I like all the things money provides, but it's just applause for providing value and changing lives. That's the true benefit for becoming a "Millionaire."

For me, it's time for a new dream - and a new vision.

Yes, I still want to make millions of dollars... but this time, *now*, instead of making a million dollars, I want to make a million entrepreneurs. A million people who like me, don't see the world the same way everyone else does. And if you're reading this book right now, you're probably one of them. You may not be chasing moths in left field or stuck in an ADHD trance, but you know you are meant for more. You probably have an idea for a business or a business and you want to know how to grow it faster, be more profitable, build an audience, become famous or flat out change the world. You have a message to share and it would be a tragedy to make the people of this great planet wait another 20 years (plus or minus a week) to get it.

And the fact of the matter is, what you'll learn in this book is much, much bigger than money in your bank account.

It's the ability to build, grow and engage an audience that follows you and your message and invests in your vision, your products and services. And repeat the process over and over again.

Welcome to the greatest moment in human history - where it's possible to connect with nearly the entire human race for free and build an engaged audience that rewards you with celebrity, fame and fortune.

Let's get started.

Chapter One: Webcasting 101, Who. What. Why.

· ·

"Every great dream begins with a dreamer. Always remember, you have within you the strength, the patience, and the passion to reach for the stars to change the world."

Harriet Tubman

· ·

Why Not You? Why not now?

Can we take a moment to talk about you? If you're reading this book, you're smart and resourceful. You're most likely an entrepreneur - or want to be. You're good at what you do, you know that. There probably isn't a problem you can't fix, a scenario you can't handle in your expertise or niche. You and your team take on customers or clients and their lives change.

But you could do better. You could be more. You could be making more.

You want more than financial security and a full schedule. You want the world to know you as the industry authority you are. More people *should* hear your wisdom. You *should* have a loyal tribe, an audience and list of people who follow you, trust you, listen for your guidance, buy your products and services. This isn't arrogance. If you could just gain more exposure, grow an audience, connect with more people, you could improve more lives. People would be healthier or happier or wealthier or all of the above.

If only you could reach them faster and more effectively…

And then, there's the added benefit that if you *could* reach more people, bigger things could happen for *your* life. As influence, impact and fame expands, so do your opportunities and the growth of your bank account. You should be able to say with confidence and conviction, "No matter what the market is doing, I am competition and recession proof." You should be so far ahead, even if the competition gained a little ground, they wouldn't even be able to see the dust you've kicked up ahead of them on the path to excellence.

But are you? This is the question that likely keeps you up at night. As you stare at the ceiling waiting for sleep to come, the question to ask yourself is, "What am I doing *right now* to build my brand, engage with a practically limitless audience who *wants* to hear from me, and encourage them to connect with me and buy my products and services?"

If webcasting isn't your answer… you could be left behind.

Now, I've been doing this long enough to know that you might still be a little skeptical, and I'm okay with that. You might have already written yourself out of this opportunity because you don't think you're good on camera. You wouldn't know what to say or you think your nose is too big.

What keeps many of my past customers from taking the first step is the fear that they'll say or do the wrong thing, embarrass or humiliate themselves or someone they care about will say they're an imposter… I get it. But that's a bad voice that's probably held you back from taking chances and risks in the past. It takes courage to produce your first webcast.

As some of my clients say, half-joking, "I have a face made for radio."

Listen…even if you're Rudolph the red-nosed reindeer, webcasting can work for you. You might think because you don't have something to sell, webcasting isn't for you. The good news? Webcasting is the fastest way to create content that can be turned into sellable products. Maybe you're concerned you don't have a list or that your social following isn't big enough.

You'll be relieved to know that if you can gather as few as 2, engaged, qualified people you've got yourself a webcast. Even if you're so non-technical you have to ask your 11-year-old-nephew how to turn on your camera. Or if your team is so small you don't even have a nephew to ask for help… webcasting will still work for you. If you think not enough time or not enough money will stop you — webcasting can give you exactly what you need, time *and* money . No matter who you are, what skills and experience you have or don't, webcasting can work for you.

In fact, let's play a little game. I like to call it, "Is this You?"

Below are three different example categories of webcasters. Take out your pen and check which one, (or more than one), sounds most like you. Lots of entrepreneurs are a mix of all of them...

The Enhancer

If you already have a business or specialty or trade experience, you are likely an Enhancer. You have been working in your field, developing your expertise, and you have lots of experience and wisdom from spending 5, 10, 25 or more years in your field. People come to you for answers because you have them. However, you are limited by the income you can earn using your current model. Perhaps you trade your time for money — you charge per hour or service. You want more. More clients, more customers, more reach, more revenue, more freedom. You've considered (or perhaps are considering for the first time as you read this) turning your knowledge into a product that can be sold anytime; while you're on vacation or in the middle of the night, people can buy what you know.

Your goal is to multiply your income, work less, become competition and recession-proof and find a way to get off the "treadmill" of trading time for money.

Here's an example of an "Enhancer", Meet Jerry:
Jerry is a 41 year old consultant who works with small business owners, helping them build mobile marketing systems to capture leads for their trade shows, help them write books to promote their products and build their brands and produce videos to promote and market their services.

Lately, Jerry is finding there are lots of competitors in his business environment that are driving the prices he can charge down and creating confusion in the marketplace so he's looking for an "edge" that can allow him to work less, charge more money and get a high-quality client who can see his value.

Although Jerry loves to consult, he dreams of himself being in front of the camera, acting as a host with his clients and producing live shows for them that can supplement or replace their trade shows, travel and traditional sales.

Jerry knows that when he starts providing Webcast services to his customers, he'll get an edge over his competitors, be able to charge a fee plus a percentage of profits when he helps his customers grow their businesses and most likely, start a local online interactive television show that he can use to start getting sponsor and advertiser support in addition to growing his consulting business.

Jerry hates the fact that he's constantly scrambling for the next project or client deal, is frustrated by the fact that he's been unable to set up a means to get monthly recurring revenue because his business is project-based.

Jerry feels stuck because in order to grow, he needs more people but doesn't want to bring on full-time employees because he doesn't want to take on overhead or risk.

For Jerry, what he loves is the idea that he could start doing weekly or monthly "shows" with his clients, get paid on a regular ongoing basis and get a percentage of sales or growth from his clients is very exciting. If he can start his own interactive live television show with sponsor support means he'll get recurring income without having to do lots of production work.

The Reinventer

You are a "reinventor" if you are someone who may have sold a business, retired or is flat-out frustrated with the BUSINESS you are in, but still loves WHAT YOU DO.

Examples of these are people in heavily regulated medical, financial and insurance industries. They LOVE to help people with their know-how and experience but spend 15%-20% of their time actually DOING what they love and instead spend more time on paperwork, bureaucracy and BS. It's often that stuff that causes them to quit or leave the profession in the first place.

A primary question Reinventors often ask or say is "if I could just DO what I love to DO without the business and bureaucracy headaches, that's what I'd spend my time on!" Instead, they're met with constant frustration.

If you have been successful at something in the past, but you're transitioning into a whole new world or field, you are likely a Reinventor. In fact, most entrepreneurs I know go through 5 or more "reinventions" during a single career. Reinventors take what they know from their area of experience and leverage that into something new, bigger, better, and more fulfilling.

Here's an example of a "Reinventor"...Meet Linda:

Linda is a 45 year old doctor, who is non-technical but is reasonably comfortable on camera. She dreams of being featured on a national TV show someday. She's an MD who has written a book or wants to, still practices 3-4 days per week but wants to grow her online presence with some kind of online video that she hopes will get the attention of broadcast television producers.

She's reached a point in her career where she realizes she's "trading time for money" and wants to get out of the daily grind of seeing patients and dealing with insurance claims. She knows the only way she can do that is with her own products, promoting her book, selling a line of supplements and changing her business model to "coach" her patients through elective packages instead of appointments.

Linda LOVES creating, helping people, doing her work and has a great community of other complementary experts in her field.

Linda is FRUSTRATED by the fact that the medical world forces her to do mountains of paperwork, deal with insurance, she's always in fear of legal issues and can't seem to break through her "glass ceiling" of business growth because she can't find or train good people fast enough to manage her practice without her babysitting it and them. She's stuck working IN her business versus ON her business.

Linda loves to present, speak, educate and teach but doesn't love to market herself but has reached a point where she knows it's necessary to get to the next step.

One of the things that holds Linda back is she doesn't feel as though she's technical enough and gets hung up on technology. She feels as though she has been screwed over by web developers, designers and production people but is just starting to realize it's mainly because she doesn't know exactly what she wants or needs and can't communicate her vision and outcome clearly.

This makes her feel "stuck" and the idea of having a Webcast and being able to put on a "show" of her own without being a techie is very attractive to her because she could do it herself, teach, communicate and talk about the things she loves most and get paid for it!

The Creator

Have you started or tried multiple businesses? You might be a serial or want-to-be-entrepreneur with more ideas than you have time. Perhaps you're retired and realize you want to get back into the game - but on your terms. Maybe you love seminars and reading ABOUT starting a business but haven't figured out where to begin or what to do?

Maybe you had or still have a business or a job and you'd like to just start from scratch and do something brand-new, either part-time or full-time.

If you lie awake at night (or wake up really early) with one great idea after another, then you're probably a Creator. Creators can't help themselves - they create! If you have a team or assistants who are constantly running around like chickens with their heads cut off, you're a Creator. The great news - the world moves off Creator's energy. Things like iPhones, airplanes, toasters, and soap that you squirt into your hand are a daily reality because of people like you.

Here's an Example of a "Creator", Meet TJ:

TJ is a 51 year old professional with a dream of turning his ideas into a line of products. Previously, he worked as a manager at a large corporation.

After "being on the road" for 20 years, dealing with 80 people in his department, TJ has realized he doesn't like the company he works for, the idea of starting a business with overhead, the stress and the fact that traditional marketing and sales don't work as well as they used to.

TJ would like to start a new business that makes at least six figures a year and eventually grow to a make couple million dollars and even sell it someday without having to work crazy hours or take on a lot of financial risk.

TJ loves the idea of being on camera and knows how to teach and train. He'd like to make a product suite that would include books, courses that can be sold online, training programs, and maybe include coaching and consulting for high-end clients.

Right now he doesn't have a prospect list or web site but is familiar with basic marketing concepts and has attended some marketing events in the past.

He loves the idea of using webcasts so he can escape much of his operationally-focused life and move towards spending 65%-80% in "creative mode" educating and being able to connect directly to an online audience from his home office or even when he's on vacation from anywhere in the world.

This shift will make him as much money or more than he's making now, accessible without all the travel, expense, hassle and complexity of the "old" company he's ready to leave.

Creators are driven by freedom - and the desire to be autonomous. To be able to do business on their terms, anytime, anyplace, full-time or part-time.

Who are you? Are you a Creator, Reinventor or the Enhancer? Perhaps a mix of two or all three. When I ask this question to my live or online audiences many of them say they are all three! If you don't recognize yourself in this description, do not fear. You might be a rare case and I can't wait to see what webcasting will do for you.

My point is, webcasting will work in any industry, across any business type and in spite of any real or perceived shortcomings. Whether you live at the top of a mountain or in your grandmother's basement, as long as you have an internet connection, a computer with a webcam, you can make it work for you.

I've witnessed individuals just like you—on the brink of reaching their full potential—explode into superstardom using this one, simple, tool. You could be next. You could be the next Tony Robbins, Dr. Oz, or Oprah of your industry.

It could be you - but there is some real urgency in getting started now. As you're reading this book right now, the power of webcasting is still underground and relatively unknown and undiscovered. Very few are tapping into the full potential and leveraging the virtually unlimited power of webcasts. You can be one of the first.

By the end of the this chapter you will know exactly what a webcast is, what they can do for you and by the end of this book you will have a step-by-step formula for producing, performing, promoting and profiting from your very own webcast.

What the Heck is a Webcast Anyway?

A "webcast" is a live or recorded online event that includes video, interactive chat and the ability to present an "order now" or "buy" button. It's like an infomercial where the host can "talk" to you while the show is happening. However, unlike an infomercial, a webcast is more targeted, infinitely more personal and essentially risk free for the producer.

A webcast DOESN'T have to include a buy button, however. They can be used for training, education, entertainment or practically any other communication, virtual meeting or community application.

A WEBINAR on the other hand, is voice with a computer screen. This is something you would do with GotoWebinar, WebEX or any number of competitive products if you do a search on Google for "webinar software."

There are five components to a webcast page:

Component One: Video
A webcast isn't an audio recording and it's not a static screen with a voiceover. One of the most unique aspects of webcasting is it's LIVE (at least the first time around—it can certainly be replayed, we'll get into that later) and INTERACTIVE. It's you, the video camera, and the thousands of people who tune in to watch you. It's very personal and intimate. It's as if you were standing in their living room or sitting with them at their desk, connecting with your audience face-to-face, one-on-one.

Component Two: Share Buttons
By adding social sharing buttons to a webcast page, we've found that by simply ASKING the audience in chat to share links, we can increase our audience by as much as 12%! If you take into account that webcasts can frequently convert 10% to 50% of an average viewing audience into buyers, this can dramatically affect your sales...at no added cost.

Component Three and Four: Audience and User Chat
A webcast has a live, interactive chat that runs to the side or below the video window This feature is the *secret sauce*

infomercials never had. When you talk to the camera, delivering your information, you can interact with your viewers in real time, by responding to the questions and comments they enter into chat. You can overcoming practically any objection and clear up any doubts your audience has.

You know how excited you get when you sign into Facebook and you see that little red "notification" icon in the corner because someone has left you a comment? Imagine that feeling x10, or x100, or x1,000 depending on how many people are online during your webcast. Watching the comments roll in on the screen is thrilling. But chat is more than just fun or entertaining...

Chat solves a serious problem—eliminating distraction! Think about it, how many windows do you have open on your screen at any given time? Or when you're watching television, how often are you also doing lots of other things; scrolling through social media, shopping online, texting, tweeting, twaddling and Facebooking. Chat keeps viewers busy. It keeps them engaged. If you use it right, chat keeps their fingers on the keyboard, eyes on the screen and their ears paying attention to YOU—exactly where you want them.

Not only that, chat becomes the most valuable superpower you could ever wish for. Have you ever wished you could read the minds of your potential customers? It's the ultimate unfair advantage every marketer and salesperson has ever wanted.

Have you ever tried to write marketing copy for your product or service and wondered if it'll actually work—wonder if your potential clients are into it or not? In webcasting, you don't have to wonder... you can simply ask questions and read the chat feed as it rolls in, real-time. Do they express their excitement when you talk about the benefits? It's working! Do they seem confused about something you thought was pretty clear? Adjust your message and try again. Never in the history of anything have we been able to gather real-time feedback. Imagine how much more effective you'll be when you can literally switch your sales pitch in the middle of it.

And if you don't know anything about how to "pitch" or sell, don't worry about that right now. I'll share my best sales secrets in an upcoming chapter.

Some of my favorite moments in my career have been participating in chat conversations with my customers, from around the world, in real time during a webcast. Even more exciting is when they show up at an event and I meet them for the first time but it feels like I'm reconnecting with an old friend... That's the power of webcasting and chat; building real intimate relationships with your customers.

It's simply the most intimate form of online communication en-masse you can do in my opinion...and a larger audience makes it more intimate because you can address and help more people at once with their constant feedback.

Component 5: Buy Button
The last element of a webcast is the buy button.

At several points during your show, you can make a button appear at the bottom of the screen so people can invest in your product or service. It's either a button, or instruction to go to a web page, text or call a phone number—some way for them to take action and buy yours or someone else's product. This component is *so* important, I actually dedicated an entire chapter to profiting from webcasts later in this book.

Those are the *Must-Have* elements of a webcast. If you're missing one, it's not a webcast. It might be a webinar. It might be a podcast. If it doesn't have video, share buttons, an audience and chat, and a buy button, it is *not* a webcast.

My guess is, before I move on, there are a few more questions you need answered. Let's get those out of the way now because you're gonna love what's coming next:

Q: What kind of technology or systems are required to do a webcast?
I'll cover all of the tech and tools in a later chapter, but the short answer to the question is as long as you have a desktop or laptop computer, webcam and microphone, you've got what you need.

Beyond that, the software you can use can be 100% free — including Google Hangouts, YouTube Live, LiveStream, uStream for broadcasting. There are low-cost systems that can be used to capture names, build a list, take orders, do chat and follow up with your leads or buyers that cost a couple hundred dollars per year.

The bottom line is you can get started for free and move up to paid tools once you're up, running and profitable.

Q: How long should my webcast be?

Great question with a simple answer—however long you want it to be. Usually no fewer than 50 minutes, but anything after that is fair game. 2 hours, 5 hours, 8 hours. As I mentioned, I did a webcast that lasted 12 hours once.

Now you might be saying, "Who the heck would watch a webcast for 12 hours?!" But over those 12 hours we averaged 3,100 viewers and sold $3.1 million dollars of products.

Could we have stopped at 4 hours? Sure. But they were still buying. Orders were coming in during the 12th hour—why would we stop?! If you were making over $100,000 per hour, would you stop talking to an audience that stuck around, loving everything you say?

So if you're asking how long should a webcast be, the short answer is: As long as they're still buying!

Q: How do I fill 50 minutes (or even 12 hours) of time?

This is the fun part! Later in the book I will give you a step-by-step guide to producing a profitable webcast including the "show-flow" (my blueprint for producing million dollar webcasts).

For now, I'll say that the options are endless:
- Step-by-step demonstrations of your products
- Examples of how people are using your products and services
- Conduct in-depth interviews with satisfied customers
- Videos of client testimonials or before and after images
- Q&A via chat is always a must (and really fun!)
- Interviewing one or a panel of experts in person or remotely
- A "pitch" or offer
- A guarantee of some sort

We've done live cooking shows, we've produced shows for financial products and services, programs about writing and publishing books, fitness programs, personal development programs and corporate training. Our clients have produced shows about real estate, QiGong, Yoga, college tuition, spiritual programs and much more. There is no end to the possibilities - if someone has written an article, book or done a podcast on a topic, it can be a webcast.

Q: Can I replay my webcast?

Absolutely! Just like an infomercial, a webcast can be repeated, but *better* than an infomercial, it can be broadcast and rebroadcast and played over and over again... and it doesn't cost you a thing!

My friend John Assaraf, star of the revolutionary movie *The Secret* and New York Times #1 Best Selling author now earns as much as $500,000 a week and sometimes more on encore replays alone (more on his incredible story later!).

Think about it for a moment; with nothing more than a mobile phone or tablet, laptop computer and a webcam, you can broadcast to a limitless audience in minutes. You can educate, demonstrate, entertain—build loyalty, trust, connection. It's fun, it's rewarding and it's FREE!

When I started doing webcasts, just a few years ago, it cost $20k a DAY. Today, it's FREE.

What Can a Webcast Do for YOU?

The simple answer is, *whatever you want*, but I understand if you want something more. So let's break this down.

A webcast can answer questions, overcome objections, demonstrate products, collect data, interview people, but more importantly it can sell things.

The 12 Benefits of Having Your Own Webcast/Online TV Show
1. Access to an international audience.
Anyone from anywhere in the WORLD can view your webcast. "Going international" in business used to cost *millions* of dollars

in staffing and training alone. Now, it costs the same to reach a middle-class mother in Wisconsin as it does to connect with a teenager in Zimbabwe with a smartphone. Free!

2. Freedom.

Webcasts can be produced from anywhere. Do your webcast from your living room or home office. Film it outside. Do one while you're on vacation—if your husband goes golfing for the day while you're in Maui, you can do a webcast from the hotel balcony. I once interviewed X-Prize Founder Peter Diamandis on the balcony of my home in La Jolla. Anywhere your phone goes is a possible location for a webcast. Not to mention, once your webcast moves to an encore or replay, you don't even have to be there. You can earn money while you sleep! (Or while you're doing something more exciting than sleep.)

3. Easily write your first (or next) book.

Have you been meaning to write a book but just hate the painstaking task of plunking out 300 pages on the computer? With webcasting you don't have to. A 4 hour webcast could easily be transcribed and edited into a 80-100 page book. We've helped hundreds of people write books using this strategy.

And if you don't think you can write a "good" book in just a few hours - I'd like to challenge that belief. Chances are, you've been teaching some big ideas or concepts for years - or even decades. Your stories and ideas work in conversations or presentations in your business. Why not just document them into a new format?

4. Sell more products and services faster and with less effort

Webcasting is significantly more efficient than traditional sales. No more traveling from meeting to meeting—you don't even have to fill your day with multiple phone calls. With webcasting you can talk to and sell to all of your potential clients at once.

5. Rapidly build a list

I often hear people say, "Mike, I can't do a webcast yet. I don't have a list." My answer is simple: put the horse in front of the cart! Webcasts are a great way to build a list. Just let the people you already know in your real and social world what you do by launching your show. You'll be surprised at what happens organically.

In an upcoming chapter, I'll share a list of free websites you can use to promote your webcast to get free traffic and visitors.

6. Passive income

One word = ENCORE. Your webcast can be playing (and making money) while you sleep, or eat, or exercise, or wash the car, or go to happy hour, or bake a birthday cake or… Why don't you make your own list. Write at the top of a piece of paper OTHER THINGS I'LL DO WHILE MY WEBCAST MAKES ME MONEY. I bet you come up with some good ideas.

Even if you don't have your own products or services, you can promote other people's products as an affiliate. I recently recorded an interview with a business owner that sells merchant services for entrepreneurs who want to accept credit cards. I played that video online and every time someone signs up for his service, I get a percentage of every transaction they do. I've been receiving over $3,000 per month in commissions for over 8 months!

7. Sell live physical events, seminars, workshops

There's a chance you're thinking, "This webcasting thing is interesting Mike, but I already do live events, workshops and seminars… and I *like* doing them. I don't need a webcast." To that I say, what better way for your potential workshop goers to get a sense for how amazing you would be in person than to see you live in a webcast. I have multiple clients who use webcasting to fill their live events and it's extremely effective at getting warm bodies in the seats.

8. REPLACE live physical events.

Maybe you produce live events, but you're sick of them. They're expensive, high-risk, grueling, and require a lot of specialized manpower to do effectively. Or maybe your events take you on the road and you'd rather spend more time at home with your family than on a plane with (sometimes gassy) strangers. Webcasting can take you out of the hotel ballroom and off the tarmac for good. Deliver the same message to more people with little help and no time away. Webcast today, dinner with your sweetheart tonight.

We use webcasts to sell and deliver live events with minimal financial risk.

9. Create content, podcasts, products and online courses.

I create all of my products now using webcasts. If I have a new concept I want to teach or a new product I want to sell, I produce a webcast on that topic. I promote it, invite people to join, I do a webcast to sell the new product and then produce a webcast to make the product! I also use webcasts to produce content for social media. For example, I can invite an audience of 1 or 1,000 to attend a special live webcast and then that webcast can be edited into 10 videos, transcribed into 10 articles and then posted on dozens of social sites and blogs. This book you're reading right now originated as several webcasts that were transcribed, cut up, rearranged and edited. Yep, you're reading a best-selling book, but you're also "reading" a webcast.

10. You don't have to be a salesperson...

You might not like the idea of being a salesperson. *"I'm not a salesperson, Mike. I just want to help people. I like to teach, not sell."* I get it. That's fine. In fact, this is perfect for you. One of the best things about webcasting is, it's your show! (Yes, you ARE an entertainer). The best thing you can do is be yourself—*your* sense of humor, *your* style of delivery. If you don't want to be all-salesy, then *don't* be. Be you. Help people. Your audience will feel the congruency of your character through the screen and those who resonate will buy. More importantly, you get instant, immediate feedback. You'll see and feel what works best for you and your audience.

11. ... you can just be a teacher.

Again, webcasting isn't about hard selling. It doesn't have to sound like the 2:00 am vacuum infomercial. Instead, it's a platform for education. Teach your viewers. Demonstrate a new product. Educate them on your new, revolutionary approach to doing something. Don't feel pressured to sell, sell, sell. They will buy if they want more of what you teach. The simple truth is great marketing is great education.

12. You can get other people to promote you.

Do you have a date and time scheduled for your webcast? Tell other influencers about it. If their audience would find value in what you teach, ask them to promote the event too. They can earn a little for the referrals (I'll explain how later) and you gain more followers (and earn more in the process). The secret to getting other people to promote you and your content is to invite them to be interviewed on your show! This is the #1 strategy to building an audience or list when you're starting from scratch.

13. BONUS Reason—Intimacy. Instant Feedback.

I was working with celebrity nutritionist and multiple New York Times Bestselling author, JJ Virgin. You may remember her from multiple PBS specials. She came to me because she wanted to get off the road and find a way to connect with her audience more effectively. After her first webcast, she turned to me and said: "I just learned more about my customers in 2 hours than I have in 10 years. All I want to do are webcasts. They're much more profitable and fun compared to my other marketing strategies.

That's the true power of webcasting. Because there is NO delay between what you say and how people react in chat. That means you can tweak, enhance and adjust your message real time.

Think an aspect of your training is crystal clear but your chat is flooded with questions asking for clarification... You can fix your explanation right then and there. If you make a pitch and your viewers are confused, they'll tell you. If they don't, just ask them more questions. You can adjust everything in real-time with a new and improved version. This kind of feedback normally takes weeks, months or even years to do with surveys and testing - and it can be done in a matter of hours with a webcast. You'll learn what excites them, what makes them laugh. No other medium allows for this kind of intimate, instant feedback.

The Three Best Things About Webcasts Are...

1. The first life you change
2. The first dollar you make
3. and knowing you can do it over and over again

Do you remember the first kiss with someone you wanted to kiss for a long time? Do you remember the electricity and intensity when your lips finally met?

That *electric high* is exactly what it feels like when your first comment appears and the first order rolls in from your webcast. There is nothing more exciting, more satisfying, more addictive than when the Buy Button appears on the screen and orders start coming in. All you'll think is "This is amazing. I want more."

In the following chapters I am going to walk you through what happens in a webcast. We'll break it down in Five Steps.

Five Steps to Creating a Kick-Butt Webcast

1. Prepare:
Webcasts begin with preparation. You need to clearly define what your outcome, "show hook" and "showflow" will be. The best webcasts are those that start with a great plan. As simple as this sounds, it's the difference between ok results and massive sales. More importantly, it's cheap to fix problems ahead of time than after you're already in production. Planning and preparation saves and makes you money.

2. Produce:

Producing is basically setting up your computer, plugging in a webcam and microphone and using free or very inexpensive software to broadcast your show. Many people let the "tech" stop them before they start. Even if you aren't tech-minded, it just takes a little bit of practice. If you remember the first time you used social media or even a web browser, it took a few minutes to get your head around the basic principles.

3. Promote:

Promotion means getting attention, building an audience and getting people to show up. If you're going to do a webcast, you needpeople watching. In an upcoming chapter, I'll teach you a few simple tricks to getting an audience to discover you, register and get engaged on your show.

4. Perform:

Once the stage is set and the audience is there, it's time to go live and put on a great show. Great webcasts are one-part influence, one-part persuasion, and one part entertainment. Once you have a great show that produces results, you can repurpose and reuse it over and over again.

5. Profit!

The last step is where the rubber meets the road. It's where you ask the viewer to do something, you get paid. Win. Win. If your goal is pure education, content creation or delivery of a product, you might think you can skip this step. Smart content creators and marketer know they're always marketing and always selling.

Opportunity of a Lifetime

Webcasting is the future of marketing, selling, teaching and training. Right now over half of the population of the planet has Internet access and can watch interactive live or recorded videos or podcasts from their smartphones, tablets, desktop and laptop computers or smart televisions and that number is only going up. There are screens everywhere and before long your face on thousands or millions of them!

Just imagine being able to sell your product to all those people at little to no cost or risk.

Imagine being the star of your own television show — where people tune in to learn from you, to chat with you, just to hear YOU give them a shout out.

Imagine being able to take your webcast recordings and create content that helps build your brand, visibility and audience working for you as an annuity.

Imagine getting paid 2 to 5 times or more than you do right now, sharing and selling what you know best and doing it in a format that isn't yucky or salesy and is congruent with who you are. You don't have to change anything about you to be wildly successful with webcasting.

Finally, imagine going out to dinner with friends or your spouse and from across the room one of your fans comes up to your table, thanks you for changing their life, and asks for a photo with you (trust me, that is an incredible feeling!).

In fact, while I was in the process of writing this book, I received these two letters:

Hi Mike,

I'm sure you don't read replies to these messages but I just wanted to express my gratitude to you. I was alone, broke and recently divorced when I was forwarded a copy of the book you wrote while you were getting cancer treatment. I felt like ending my life because the depression was so bad. But then I read your book cover to cover. And I realized I could do it. I could pull myself up.

I enrolled in the Publish and Profit program on nothing but faith that I would be able to pay for it somehow. You have no idea how much I've gained. No one teaches you this stuff.

Today I am on my way to publishing my book myself. I even designed and built my own website. This may not seem like a big deal since you do this kind of stuff every day...but for me with no self confidence and no self esteem, it's huge.

I just wanted you to know that you helped me more than you can ever know. And I'm so grateful to you, what you've created, and your mission. I'm glad you beat cancer and inspired me with your story. Thank you.

With love and blessings,

Katy K.P.

Editorial Note: The product Katy is describing is called "Publish and Profit" - you can learn more about it at www.PublishAndProfit.com.

Here's another one...

Dear Mike Koenigs,

As you have said at events, TELL YOUR STORY and I want to share mine with you. Last year I went to an event that Joe Polish was hosting and you were in the crowd. You were the most humble person in the room that day. You told the group how easy it is to publish a #1 bestselling book and more importantly you demonstrated it before our eyes. I was so impressed I went home and subscribed to your email list.

Over the following months after that event, I went through some major life changes and I decided to sell my 3 businesses that I owned for 8 years. I had lost all drive to be an entrepreneur and wore the heavy crown of responsibility that comes with it. On top of that my husband and I decided to divorce because we no longer want to be together and I am left with 2 kids, a large home and needed a job.

My new boss is the "Elvis" of Dentistry and has been on the lecture circuit for 25 years. He has a book coming out in October. We needed to do a little marketing, build his audience and following. When you sent an email invitation to attend your next live event, I asked my boss if I could go to get marketing ideas and he said yes!

Within 15 minutes of being in your event, I realized I was not attending for my job but for myself! I took notes, I shook hands, I went to lunch and discussed ideas with people and I forgot all about my 40 hr job. It was AMAZING. When I flew home Sunday night I brought back home with me the ENTREPRENEURIAL Spirit I had abandoned last summer.

Within 2 weeks of being home, I invested in your system and jumped in and implemented. I watched every video, did every step, joined the Facebook group using my newly divorced name and started creating a new life based upon a NEW ENTREPRENEURIAL dream. I wrote a book about what I know so well, opening a niche business. You see I owned the ONLY WOMEN'S ONLY CrossFit gyms in the world. Women spend the most money on fitness and most women do not wish to be intimidated by young men lifting heavy stuff at the typical CrossFit gyms.

I am BACK and I am ALIVE AGAIN because of you and your system! I cannot wait for my book to be released on April 22nd. I want to do two things with this book launch. First test your awesome system from start to finish so I can take the next step and become a book marketing consultant. I want to be able to tell clients I DID IT and it changed my life and I can help them change their lives too. I would love to reach out and help others WRITE THEIR STORY and use it to promote themselves or as a powerful business card. Second I would like my book to be "my" business card and I would like to once again encourage others to grab their place in their market like I have the WOMEN'S market in the fitness industry.

I can't thank you enough for helping me realize my dream and I know I will be able to quit my unrewarding job and be an AWESOME Entrepreneur again!

Thank you so much!

Rebecca F.

This is the fuel that feeds my soul. You can get these too....

All you have to do is take the first step. And lucky for you, that's what the next chapter is all about: Step One of your first webcast, Prepare.

FREE - WEBCASTS ABOUT WEBCASTS

Nearly everything in this book is demonstrated step-by-step for you in regular bi-weekly and recorded webcasts with the author of this book, Mike Koenigs. He'll guide you through everything you need to know to start or grow a business using webcasts in a fast-paced, fun, interactive format and answer your questions.

Register right now at www.WebcastProfitToolkit.com

Chapter 2:
Step One - Prepare

"Fortune favors the prepared."

Louis Pasteur

One of the best things about a webcast is, with very little preparation time, you can put together an event that can generate significant income in a few hours. Some of my students and customers have gotten started and produced their first shows in only 48 hours that have produced sales the exceeded $100,000 the first time.

All it takes is clarity on three essential elements:
- Market
- Message
- Media

Let's go through each of these step-by-step:

Market

The very first step in preparing for your webcast is to get razor-sharp, laser-focused, crystal clear on **who** your Market is. Who are you going to sell to? Who do you want to buy your products? Who needs them? Who wants them? *And*, does the market you're pursuing have a consistent behavior of spending money buying products like yours?

Here are a few things to consider about your Market as you prepare your live webcast:

Don't Sell to People who Can't Buy.

This is a no brainer. I've found one of the biggest mistakes new entrepreneurs make is starting a business to help broke or *broken* people. Next, they wonder why they don't make money. Here's the cold, hard, sugar-free truth. It doesn't matter how great your product is, if your audience doesn't spend money on the kind of

43

thing you're selling, you'll go broke and be broken too. I hear it all the time, "I'm selling to people who are cheap and they don't have any money..."

That's your problem, not theirs! Don't make a business selling to broke or broken people because that isn't a business. It's a charity. Your goal should be to sell to an accessible market, with a lot of money, with a big pain they've repeatedly spent money on to solve. They already need to WANT what you have to sell. Once you've successfully set up a business with cash flow, you can give your money away to broke or broken people. Otherwise, you'll end up broke and broken too.

Focus on a Entering a *Crowded* Niche

When it comes to preparing your product and preparing your webcast, here's the game plan I want you to follow: enter a crowded market—one that's already filled with products, but one you can narrowly identify and focus in on a niche. Sounds crazy, right? Focus on *fewer* people? Doesn't that mean less money? A narrow niche equals more money *because* you can clearly and succinctly state what your product will do for them.

To show you what I mean, let's look at two sample products/webcasts. You tell me which one you think will make more money?

Door #1:

> I'm selling happiness. I discovered how to be happy.
> I wrote a book and am going to call it,
> "The Happy Code: How to be Really Happy."

or Door #2:

> I'm selling leads. I have a simple, repeatable 3-step system for generating leads for realtors. My product is called "Guaranteed San Diego Home Buyer Leads: How to Get 500 Leads for San Diego Realtors for Less than $500 in Just 7 Days, Guaranteed or Double Your Money Back."

Which one do you think is the better product/offer? One could apply to "everyone," one applies to a specific few. But I'm sure, even as you read it, you know it's the second one that gets it right. It's a great offer! It's for a very specific audience, it promises a specific deliverable in a specific time frame with a guarantee right in the title.

The Happy Code isn't a product. "Everyone" isn't a market. You can find articles about being happy for free online. Now, if the author wrote a book, "The Happy Code; The Five-Step Breast Cancer Survivor's Guide for Women 45 and Older to Smile Again in Just 20 Minutes." *That* would be a great offer! If the book was for breast cancer survivors who've had double mastectomies and are struggling to find happiness in their new bodies—that would be a winner! That's a narrow niche, but there's a lot of women who have had mastectomies, they're reachable and will be motivated to buy the book - and most likely an audio book or course to go along with it.

The only time a "generic" or general product will sell is if you're already a celebrity or have a celebrity endorsement. When you're building a platform, you need to be specific. You need to appeal to the WANTS and DESIRES of your specific, focused, target audience.

Why Would Someone Sit and Watch a 4-8 Hour Webcast?

You are *not* your market. AND! Your market isn't you. You've already solved the problems your market has... that's why they're coming to you! You figured it out.

They are coming to you because you have the answer—and solution. If you are thinking to yourself right now, "I would never sit on a webcast about "my topic" for 2 or 8 or 10 hours so why would anyone else?!?" you've got your thinking all wrong. If your market believes those 8 hours with you will change their life and solve a big problem, you bet they'll tune in and stick around! It's a huge disservice to your market and the people who need your message to think of them on the same plane as you—they're not, it's your job to get them there.

Message

Once you're clear on your market, it's time to focus on your message. This is the actual bread and butter of what you will be performing during your webcast.

As you are preparing your message, here are the things to consider.

1. What **giant problem** does your product fix? Does your market have a consistent behavior of spending money buying products like yours, being good customers, and are they accessible? Remember, they better be online (which most people are), they better have money, and it's ideal if they have already spent money on products like yours. Do they WANT what you have to offer or do you have to explain everything to them?

2. Does your product work? (fair question).

3. Has it worked for others? If so, how many case studies or success stories do you have? If you only have one, that's okay. I would even go so far as to say if you're just starting out and you have an anecdotal success story, that can work too. In other words, you can tell a story about how a celebrity or a well-known authority figure has used something like your product/system to get results. You can even quote compelling scientific data or evidence.

4. Pictures or videos, before and after, case studies, stories, or just anecdotes are all great to use as you develop your message. Do you have lifestyle videos or photos? Put 'em in there! Warning: The FTC says you can't make financial claims or specific health claims on video. You can make an implied or lifestyle statements. Note that I'm NOT an attorney, I don't play one on the internet and I'm not giving you legal advice so check with an attorney :)

5. How quickly can your customer get results and are they repeatable? Is it a one-time use? Is this a multi-time? Is it a lifestyle product? These are all message worthy points to make in your program.

6. Can you demonstrate the product? Awesome if you can! Going back to classic infomercial days, can you show step-by-step how your product works, who it's for and what it does? Can you demonstrate a before and after? Can you show someone using it and getting a result in real time? If you have a physical product, just open it up,

talk about each component and display it on a table and describe why each element is important to getting the results you promise.

7. Last but not least; if this section is making your brow sweat a little, don't fret. Even if you don't have any client testimonials. Even if no one has ever tried your product or system... Did it work for you? Did it change your life? Is this your big Why? If so, and if you can tell that story in a compelling way, that's all you need. We call this "mess to success" - and your story can be all you need to be successful.

Media

After you've considered your market & message, next you have to determine where your audience hangs out. This is a freebie for you — your audience, your market is going to meet you online in a live webcast. Now, if your market doesn't have a computer, or doesn't know how to watch an online video, or thinks the internet is some strange voodoo... as far as webcasting is concerned... you need to find a new market.

The other thing to consider in terms of media is — are there other media channels, beside online that your market hangs out? Are they on social? Do they watch TV? Are they on YouTube? Facebook? Pinterest? Instagram? LinkedIn? Are there groups of them? I tell you this because once you know where they hang out, ask yourself if you know an *influencer* who runs in their circle, or who they admire, who would be willing to endorse you? Do you know a celebrity, belong to an association, have an in with an organization who would "up" your credibility with your market by saying, "Kendra is the world's authority on blank and she has something she wants to give you — here's a place where you can get her latest book for free for the next 48 hours."

That's it! That's all you need to prepare for your webcast. Get clear on those three items: Market, Message, Media.

As a matter of fact, that's an important point. There is one thing that will kill your webcast... inaction. Don't spend the next six months "preparing,"... spend the next six hours MAX. Then move on to the next step. Webcasting is so simple, overthinking it will kill it before it starts.

CASE STUDY: Brad Costanzo — A MAN OF ACTION

Brad Costanzo is a friend of mine. We belong to a mastermind group and had a conversation about all the great opportunities possible with webcasting, Brad committed to doing one. At the time, he didn't have a list of his own, but worked with a client who did. He decided to set up a free webcast with that client to answer questions.

The next day, Brad's client invited several hundred people to attend their first webcast and about 300 showed up. Not a bad crowd! For four hours, Brad and his client answered questions the people submitted in chat. They taught, they shared, they conversed. Brad didn't really have an agenda, or a "showflow" (which we'll discuss later), they just implemented and followed their instincts and some general guiding principles I shared with him.

Over the next four hours, they made several offers to the audience—one was an offer for a $397 training program and a chance to speak with a consultant about starting and growing a business with real estate with no money down. The offer for that program was a coaching program with a $20,000 price tag.

Brad and his client closed six figures in sales within two days of completing the webcast. By the time they finished following up with interested attendees nine days later, their sales were $193,764!

Remember, Brad did this webcast his first time without a list of his own with no agenda and without "death-by-over-preparation". Brad Costanzo just went for it and made hundreds of thousands of dollars over the course of four hours of time.

Brad recorded a testimonial for me. Here's the story as he tells it:

"Hey Mike, I've got to tell you, the marathon webcast that you were talking about the other night in our Mastermind really inspired me. That was Tuesday night. Wednesday we decided to go for it. Thursday we did an 8 hour, live webcast where we sold multiple products and I can't

believe it—we actually had a 6 figure day!

Now, what was crazy about this—within 18 hours after our conversation, we had this thing ready and rockin. We had no idea what we were doing, there was no strategy whatsoever except get online, be authentic and pull in as many offers as we could. We emailed people once the night before and again before the show started. I told them, "Look, we don't know what's going to happen. It's going to be crazy, but let's just go for it."

It worked really smoothly. It was fun, it was exciting. I lost my voice a little bit, but everybody loved the show. We got tons of feedback, we've got a great recording. We sold $30,000 in the first few hours, then sales just kept on coming in and coming in. Everything from product sales, to coaching applications to coaching sales and everything else. Within two days after finishing the show, we closed over $100,000 in product sales.

I had no idea that it would work as well as it did and big thanks to you, man. You inspired me and, hopefully, you're inspiring a lot of other people to give it a try. I think we're seeing a new big trend in this industry and I think it'll be a good one. Thanks a lot man."

I spoke with Brad nine days after the event ended. Their total sales, as a result of the webcast, was estimated to be $193,764. Not bad for a first try!

Chapter 3:
Step Two - Produce

· ·

*"Whatever course you decide upon, there is always someone
to tell you that you are wrong. There are always difficulties
arising which tempt you to believe that your critics are right.
To map out a course of action and follow it to an
end requires courage."*

Ralph Waldo Emerson

· ·

It happens too often—I'll meet someone who is clearly an established star in their field (or a rising star with a ton of potential). They're great at what they do, people like them, trust them, and do what they tell them to do (like buy stuff they recommend). They have a message, they know their market and they know they're not maximizing their knowledge or skill. As the conversation continues, I introduce the idea of webcasting.

After describing it, I might get a deer-in-the-headlights look (I grew up in Minnesota, I know that look when I see it!) followed by a litany of reasons about why webcasting wouldn't work for them. Sometimes they're concerned about performing on camera, which we'll get to in the next chapter, but most of the time they're simply overwhelmed with the unknowns of putting a webcast together.

I am going to put those fears to rest once and for all. Producing a successful webcast can be as simple a paint by numbers. It's a repeatable system that produces consistent results.

I am going to give you a formula for webcasting that you can drag and drop yourself into in less than a day. I'll teach you what a showflow is, how it will help you and give you access to some examples. And finally, I'll give you a crash course in the basics of the tech stuff—you don't have to a nerd to get a show up and running.

The Webcast Show Formula

Behind every great webcast is a well thought out formula for engaging, educating, and selling the viewers. After doing nearly 1,000 online events, my team and I have developed a formula for producing profitable webcasts. This formula can be turned into a "showflow" that can be used for a webcast of any length and across any industry. If you don't get anything else out of this book, this formula will give you a lot of insight and inspiration and will save you a lot of time, frustration and heartache.

10-20 minutes before the Webcast goes live

10 minutes before you start, put a photo up on the screen that indicates something is about to happen. It can be as simple shot of your logo, or a screen that says "The Webcast Will Begin at the Top of the Hour" You can also get more advanced—we sometimes put up testimonial videos or funny clips... the most important thing is, when your viewers arrive, you want them to know they're in the right place and the show will be starting soon.

Live! First 10 Minutes to Preframe the Audience

Once the webcast goes live, spend the first ten minutes chatting and building rapport. Talk a little about who you are, what you're going to talk about, tell your audience why you're excited they've joined you, and get the interactive chat activated and engaged.

These first 10 minutes are the warm up. Talk to the people in chat. Welcome each person who joins by name. Ask them questions. Encourage them to participate. Mention giveaways if you're going to do a raffle. No content, no selling, just visiting and building rapport and excitement.

This also gives some of the latecomers a chance to show up so they aren't lost once you get going.

30 minutes: 3 Concepts/Training Cycles or "Pods"

The next thirty minutes are the bulk of your webcast—this is where the content is.

You are going to choose 3 concepts to teach/train your audience on. Each concept should take you 7 to 10 minutes to present and should be packed with real and valuable content. This isn't about filling time with fluff—you are one click away from your viewer closing the page and watching a cat video on YouTube instead of you.

Of course, as you're teaching your concept, you will also be "seeding the sale"—making them want more from you (aka, buying your product). We'll discuss the concept of seeding later on.

Separate each content segment (or pod) by sprinkling some Q&A in between. Interact with your audience. Enjoy yourself and appreciate your audience.

Let's do a quick check in… if you're following the formula, you'll see we're now 40 minutes into your show. Time to make an offer and earn some money…

10 to 20 minute Close
After the bulk of the content, it's time to insert a close (also known as a pitch). If you've been doing a great job teaching, educating, connecting and engaging, the people in chat are going to by typing in messages like "how can I get started?" or "what do I need to do to get going right now?" or "can you help me do this?"

That's your signal to tell your audience about your offer—what makes your product so incredible, why it is the solution to the problems they have or the issues you just discussed in the content section, what special bonuses they'll get if they act fast—basically why buying your product is a no-brainer. Tell them how to buy, where to click, and then tell them to post it in chat once they've placed the order so you can congratulate them.

And that's it.

That is the basic formula for every great webcast.

Now, if you're doing the math and counted only 60 minutes total and are wondering how a 60 minute formula turns into an 8 hour event, the answer is simple: repeat. Start back at the top.

After you make the offer, go back to chatting with your viewers. Talk to them about what's coming up and why they should stick around. Review the three concepts. If you can, teach three new concepts. If you don't have that much, not to worry, re-teach what you just taught them. Then move to another 10 to 20 minute close. There's nothing wrong with repetition.

People come and go. Some will stay for the whole thing and leave when you start over, others will join part way through, some will watch the same thing over and over again because they like you! If you have an encore or replay, many of the people who didn't buy the first time will return because they want to be convinced they're making the right decision.

Optional (Recommended) Inserts

Of course, while you *can* do a webcast with just those components, it's ideal if you have more variety and more value to give. Here are some high-value and highly effective segments to add into your webcast if you can.

Make sure you make an offer and "close" at least once an hour— preferably every 50 minutes.

Interview with an authority or celebrity

Can you interview a niche celebrity? Is there someone in your industry or speciality who you could interview? Someone who would add credibility to what you teach and build the case for what you offer? (Bonus points if they have a list of their own because more people will gather to watch and you can build a list from their list!) Find an expert and interview them for 10 to 20 minutes. Better yet? Find several experts and interview all of them - one per hour or so... you just extended the length and the value of your webcast by letting someone else do the talking! And you might also be surprised at how easy it is to access authorities and celebrities.

Product success story

Time to make your happy customers famous! If you have clients who have worked with you or, better yet, have used the product you're offering with success, get them on the webcast! You can have them join live or via a split screen. Ask them to share their experience from start to finish—what they were struggling with, how you and your product solved that problem, and the success and happiness they've experienced as a result. A couple 10 to 20 minute product success stories will go a long way both in keeping your audience engaged and increasing their desire to buy!

Prizes, raffles, giveaway, and bonuses

Throughout the webcast, include different giveaways. Ask a question about something they should have learned during the webcast and whoever answers the question correctly in chat first wins! We've given away Apple watches, Apple TVs, Kindle Fires, Google ChromeCasts, LIVE event tickets, bonus training and complementary products! Giveaways are fun, interesting and exciting. You'll be shocked how long people will stick around to win something.

SALES KILLER WARNING:

One CRITICAL thing is NEVER give away or raffle the product you are selling. If you do this, people won't buy because they're going to "wait to see if they win". I've witnessed many business owners make this mistake - they see their product and offer is getting interest and attention but they don't make any sales! The process of giving away your product devalues you and your brand too. Only give away complimentary, non-competitive products that add value and don't confuse the buyers.

And that's it. Repeat those segments over and over again for as long as people are buying your product and you will have yourself an 8 hour webcast before you know it.

Showflow

Once you determine the various components of your webcast, your next step is to put those pieces together in one coherent document that will serve as your guide, your map, your webcast *bible*. This document is called the showflow.

A showflow is exactly what it sounds like; it's the flow and structure of your show. It includes the segment content and length, offers, what appears on graphic overlays, giveaways, special props and/or considerations, important phone numbers, and even the website addresses for the various checkout pages. Nothing is left for guesswork. Everything is there. The showflow is used internally—for yourself and your team if you have one—so everyone knows in advance what is going to happen every single minute of the time you're on screen.

Think of it this way: If the person in charge of making the webcast run smoothly was hit by a bus on the way to filming, the show would go on... because you have a showflow.

EXPERIENCE A SHOWFLOW

The best way to learn a showflow is to experience one by attending a live or recorded webcast. You'll see exactly how a program "opens up", builds audience rapport, teaches three lessons, involves an audience with chat and how an offer can be made. At the end of the presentation, you'll receive an opportunity to get a copy of the presentation to download and model for your own webcast

Details are at www.WebcastProfitToolkit.com

The Techie Stuff

One of the most frequently asked questions I get is "what kind of technology, equipment and services should I use to do webcasts?"

And unfortunately, this is where most people get hung up, confused and overwhelmed because it only represents 10% of what it takes to make a successful and profitable webcast.

I'm going to answer the question about equipment and software after first saying: webcasts are 90% psychology and 10% technology.

The psychology of a successful webcast is in this entire book. Right now I'll cover the tech for you - and invite you to join me for a free webcast where I discuss this further.

This is divided into "Basic", "intermediate" and "Advanced" - and that includes different prices for the systems as well.

All you really need to make a webcast work is a computer, webcam or camera, microphone and some kind of service for broadcasting your video signal. Next, you need some way to capture registrations, follow up, display chat and push sales buttons.

Note: There are apps available for iPhones and Android phones like Periscope, Meerkat and Facebook Mentions that technically allow you to do "webcasts". However, I personally don't consider them to be "real" webcasting solutions simply because they don't allow you to schedule live events with registration pages, email or mobile text follow up, true live interactive chat, buy buttons or replay capabilities

Basic (no registration or follow up) - Free to $200
Here are the basic things you'll need to get started:
1. Google Hangouts (free)
2. A laptop or desktop computer with a webcam and microphone

Optional, but recommended:
- Logitech c930e (about $100)
- Blue Nessie microphone (about $70)
- Headset for interviews (about $10)

This is a screen capture from Google Hangouts straight from the webcam on my laptop with poor room lighting. Note the "backwards" lower 3rds. This looks correct on your audience's computers!

With this basic setup, you can broadcast to 1, 10, 100 or 100,000 people at once completely free of charge. With the on-screen chat, you can take questions and respond to your audience or send links to special offers.

With this setup, although it's free, you'll need to set up your own web pages to register guests, an autoresponder to follow up and remind them and your own shopping cart to take orders.

I recommend you use a good microphone like the Blue Yeti or Nessie (not a headphone style microphone) and an in-ear headset you can wear so you look "normal" on camera.

Other solutions that have a monthly cost include uStream and LiveStream that do essentially the same thing as YouTube Live which is free. They do have some specific features that can make them better for producing live events and seminars – just visit the web sites for features and benefits

Intermediate (add $297 per year and up)
Your next step up is to add the following capabilities for your webcast events:

- **Send follow up and reminder emails** and texts to get more people to show up

- **Integrate polls and surveys** to learn more about your audience

- **Social sharing** to organically grow your audience

- **Countdowns and timer** controls to insert scarcity and deadlines

- **"Push" sale buttons** to appear when you make an offer to get the audience to buy

- **Fully integrated chat with moderation**, curse filters and chat exports so you can control "haters" and trolls if they show up on a live event

- **Playback of encore presentations** for replays and automated sales so you don't have to repeat yourself

- **Charge for webcasts** if you want to collect money without having to set up a shopping cart

- **Team management controls** so you can get help from other people remotely to manage chat, polls, shopping cart so you can focus on content

- **Metrics and reporting** that show you a full dashboard so you can determine the profitability of each show

One of the most affordable solutions that is easy to use and provide these capabilities and much more is WebinarJam Studio. The software is easy to setup and use, even for one person.

EasyWebinar and WebinarIgnition are two other solutions that are plugins for Wordpress websites that I've tested and used. Although these require some setup, they are fully integrated and hosted on your web site so you aren't stuck using someone else's service.

NERD ALERT! I'm going to get a bit techie here...don't despair if this doesn't make sense, you'll learn this stuff once you get immersed in the world a little and you don't need to know this to get started.

Intermediate with Upgraded Video ($500+)
The next step is to upgrade the quality of your video by graduating and adding a "real" video camera and a good lighting kit.

Although upgrading from a webcam to a "real" camera might seem a bit complicated at first, it's a one-time only thing and is actually easy to learn when you just dive in and do it. Improving your video quality yields massive rewards - your audience will see how much better your productions look and this will affect your brand and your ability to charge premium prices for your products.

This is done by adding a camcorder or video-capable DSLR video camera with an HDMI output, the necessary cable and a video interface box that converts an HDMI connection and signal into something that connects to a USB or Thunderbolt connection.

The best solution I've found for converting HDMI to USB is from a company called MageWell and can be found on Amazon for $300. If you have more than one USB connection on your computer, you can get multiple boxes so that you can set up a multi camera system.

This interface is the most hassle-free because it doesn't require that you download or install software drivers and works with Google Hangouts, Skype or any software that works with a webcam.

For HDMI to Thunderbolt conversion, BlackMagic Design has several interfaces available. One is called the "Intensity Shuttle" (also available with USB interface), another is called "UltraStudio Express" and "UltraStudio Mini Recorder".

There are a variety of models available and they CAN work well but I've consistently had issues with these devices because BlackMagic constantly updates their drivers, the devices often require that you reset or unplug them, they don't always work as a webcam replacement and in general, are a major pain in the butt.

The bottom line is they're professional quality products but if you're going to use them, you want to set up a stable, dedicated computer that is ONLY used for production and know that a software update or upgrade may make the current drivers suddenly not work and require that you update and tweak your machine. This isn't a good thing when you have an event scheduled to run in 30 minutes and when you test your gear learn you have to reset and debug your systems.

With regards to cameras, I'm a big fan of Canon Camcorders because you can easily connect an external microphone or mixer. Buy the best camcorder you can afford - they start at about $300 and go up.

You can also use DSLR cameras that allow for continuous HDMI output without overlays. That means you can turn off the on-screen menus and the camera doesn't shut off after shooting video for a long period of time. You'll need to do some research to find the right camera for you. These cameras generally sell for $700 and more depending on the lens you choose.

In my Webcast Profit Toolkit product, I keep a running list of cameras and equipment in a "Video Equipment Buyer's Guide" that is updated regularly and videos that show you how to set up the gear.

For a light kit, all you need is a basic 3-4 "softbox" kit that can be either fluorescent or LED lights with stands. You'll spend between $150-$1,500 or more for a basic kit.

Chapter 4:
Step Three - Promote

"Heroes must see to their own fame. No one else will."

Gore Vidal

There's no point in doing a webcast if no one is there to participate. The third step to webcasting is promoting the event so you have an audience ready to learn, chat and buy.

CASE STUDY: Lori Barr - Playing the Numbers Game

Not long ago I spoke with one of my favorite customers, Lori Barr. She's an implementer. She has a regular job as a radiologist but has been studying marketing for years. She's written a book and created some products too.

As I was writing this book, Lori went out on a limb and did her very first webcast. Because she didn't have any experience in promoting, only two people showed up. She was a little bummed. But then one of them bought her product for $297. She was really excited! A 50% conversion rate is incredible especially on her first try!

Now all she needs are more people who sign up and show up!

The point of this story is it's not important that you have a big list or audience to do your first webcast. What's important is that you just get started and DO IT.

CASE STUDY: Tristan & Sabrina Trescott - Success with QiGong

One of my favorite brand-new clients is a husband and wife team. They're absolutely adorable. They teach QiGong - if you don't know what it is, look it up on Google. It's a form of Chinese movement and energy exercise that looks a bit like TaiChi.

Neither Tristan nor Sabrina are technical and they have a small list of prospects and customers they've built over several years of speaking, posting on Facebook and attending live events.

They attended one of my training programs about webcasting and made a commitment to do their first webcast 48 hours after the event ended. They offered a free QiGong webcast workshop to their list and posted the event to some of the sites I recommend in this book.

On their webcast, they offered a live physical training workshop for a deposit of $1,000 (the event cost more than that). They had a five-figure day and closed 11 sales at $1,000 each.

And at their live training event, the majority of those people who attend sign up for more expensive products.

What was their strategy for success?

Showing up. Being real and authentic. Answering questions. A service mindset.

And making an offer.

Here's Tristan and Sabrina - don't they look like a great couple?

This chapter is dedicated to teaching you the essential elements of promoting a webcast. Just like Lori Barr, Tristan and Sabrina Trescott, you can have success when you just get started and go LIVE and you don't need a huge list or full house to succeed.

The Ultimate Promotional Strategy

When it comes to promoting your webcast, the old adage is still true—Content is King. The more content you have, the more mediums you can publish to, the more channels you're on, the more people you can reach. Later in this chapter I am going to give you my _Top 10 Ways to Promote Your Webcast_ and every single one of them requires content.

So where do you find content? Truth is, you can't _find_ it; you have to create it. My secret to creating unlimited content is something I've helped a lot of people do. My good friend and marketing guru, Joe Polish came up with a great name for a content strategy, "A Riff Kit".

Your Content "Riff Kit"

Content Riffing is simple (and fun). All it requires is that you sit down and brainstorm a list of all the things you talk about or communicate to prospects or clients. This would include short speeches or talks you've given. Common questions you answer for patients. Or even rants you make that get attention and interest in social settings—elements of what you do that you are particularly passionate about.

Think of a riff as a small, bite-sized piece of your expertise—small things you could talk about for a minute or two each. You likely have hundreds of them. Each riff is an opportunity for rapidly creating content.

For example, if you're in the nutrition business, here's a simple fill-in-the-blanks template.

You might come up with a list of the 5 foods that are killing you right now. It could be The 5 Things Every _____ Should Know to _____, or the 7 Mistakes Every _____ Makes.

Make a list of these ideas, keeping in mind that no riff is too small and each has the potential to become something much, much bigger.

So when I need to make content for a webcast or videos to put online, I just turn on the camera and record a riff! Riffs can be reused in speeches, webcasts, podcasts, online articles, sales events, blogs...or anywhere. It's like a LEGO™ construction kit for your business!

I put all of my Riffs in a Google Doc or use Evernote so I can access them anytime.

In fact, here are a few of my Riffs as examples:

1. **You Everywhere Now:** This is a big idea that you can create content once, distribute it everywhere and in every format and be seen, heard, read, viewed on any device anywhere, anytime on demand. That little riff started as a 30-second hook, then turned into a 3-minute talk, then a 10-minute talk, a book, a 2-hour speech, then the basis of a multimillion dollar product launch, and is now becoming a book and a brand in and of itself with products all its own! All from a little bite-sized idea,

2. **Publish and Profit:** : My belief that you can take any content, any presentation, any speech, transcribe it, edit it, publish it on Amazon, and become a #1 Bestselling Author in as little as a week. Itstarted out as a riff idea, the basis of my first book and now... Well *now* it's created hundreds of successful authors; people who otherwise would not have written books and now are best-sellers. That little riff became an entire franchise worth over four million dollars and is impacting people all over the world.

3. **The Lavalier Loop:** How to put on a Lavalier microphone like the pros so you look and sound like a video or television professional.

4. Another riff I'm working on is *Cancerpreneur: 10 Lessons I Learned When I was Given the Gift of Cancer.* If you don't know my personal story, I was diagnosed with stage 3a cancer. The treatments put me on a major path of personal growth and gratitude. It also brought a lot of people who had gone through cancer treatment themselves who were survivors who became customers!

In this instance, I'm using a personal hook. I'm taking the most frequently asked question I get, "What did you learn from your experience of having and surviving cancer? How did it rock your world and affect you?" and answering it in such a way that my answer becomes content. What's interesting is, after a little bit of research, I found that there are very few tools and resources available for entrepreneurs who get cancer; how to deal with it, how to communicate with their families, how to survive it, how to manage their businesses when it's unmanageable.

That one experience could become an entire franchise itself with opportunities to partner with the American Cancer Institute or the societies or organizations to cross-promote and impact a whole new group of people.

Those are just a few (from hundreds!) of the riffs that came to me and my guess is, you're already thinking about your own possible content riffs. I encourage you to sit down with a piece of paper right now and brainstorm. Write down all the possibilities then prioritize them based on what audience with money would be most interested. Even the smallest, bite sized piece can turn into a content-rich, audience-building, promotion empire.

Once you have your content, it's time to put it out there to get people to your webcast. Here is my foolproof list of promotional options for getting your market **engaged, online and excited about your live web event.**

Mike's Top 10 Favorite Ways and Places to Promote Webcasts

1. Existing Customers/List
These are the people who already know you and love you. They've been following you for a week or a decade and they're always stoked when you show up in their inbox. This is always the place to start when promoting your own webcast.

Don't have a list...or you think your list is too small?

Think again.

Everyone I know has a list. From former Presidents all the way down to your drunk Uncle Tony. Don't believe me? Ok, just look at your Facebook page. Is anyone following you there? Scroll through the contacts in your phone. Chances are you have at least 100 people and probably more like 250 in your list of contacts.

A bunch of those people will not only attend your event, but they'll probably tell others about it too (even Uncle Tony).

You probably also has a list of existing customers - these can be clients you've worked with, people who have purchased your products, your patient list, people you've sold homes to, anyone you've done business for or with.

Now, assuming you have an email list, I recommend mailing at least three emails before the show and at least one email after the show.

Here is how a typical message sequence flows:

    I. 2-3 days before the show: send an announcement and invitation

    II. The morning of the show: send a reminder

    III. When the show goes live: send a "We're LIVE" email

    IV. The afternoon (or day after) the show: send a replay link and/or reminder of the offer

Below are 4 "sample" emails. They're actually real emails we have send to hundreds of thousands of people and generating a half a million dollars in sales (or more). They promote a webcast on "How to Run a Profitable Webcast." So check out the emails below and then go to www.WebcastProfitToolkit.com to see the emails, promotion, and show recording.

Note: these emails have been written with the assumption that someone else is mailing to promote our show. We always provide our JV [Joint Venture] affiliates with all the promotional copy they need so they don't have to do any work aside from sending pre-made emails that already work

I. 2-3 days before the show: send an announcement and invitation

SUBJECT: Secrets will be exposed. (You need to do whatever you can to make this.)

Hey <name>,

It's not often we are able to get this kind of expert to share what is working NOW in their business.

And it is BIG!

We had a chance to meet with the **industry expert** *the other day in his office and he showed us behind the scenes of what he is doing in his business and we were frankly in love with every bit of it.*

On top of that he showed us case studies of a few people that he worked with (<u>These are folks that have gone one to become HUGE Authorities in their industry</u>) that had incredible results when you his system.

(And practically no one else is doing this!)

BAD NEWS- *He is almost completely unavailable for the next 4 months.*

GOOD NEWS - *We asked him if he would do a <u>special webinar</u> for our best customers (YOU) and he agreed. (I think it helped because we also shared some of our great ideas with him.)*

Bottom line... **YOU WIN**.

Who is the expert?

No other than Mike Koenigs. A leader in branding, how to become a #1 bestselling a author, making people famous, building a list, getting exposure, free traffic and free press.

Mike Koenigs wrote THE book on webcasts (you get that for free BTW), **and he's also the guy who built (and sold) Traffic Geyser and Instant Customer to a publicly-traded company this past year.**

And this is HUGE:

He's a veteran of dozens of 6-figure and 12 (count em') *7-figure launches* **based on webcasts**.

What does all this mean to you?

It all means **you'll see exactly how to get more TRAFFIC, more LEADS, and more CUSTOMERS! He's going to share his biggest secrets about how to create a profitable business quickly and easily.**

Mike will show his blueprint on how YOU can now create your own media network, TV channel, and following on your own, without having to rely on producers, publishers, and pushers (i.e. the bots at Facebook).

This is amazing and **so fresh** *we can't wait to get started on it ourselves and are happy to for you to be among the first to see it.*

This is true for you...

...even if you're afraid of being on camera.

...even if you hate technology.

...and even if you really don't like selling.

"But, (Your Name) this sounds so HARD..."

It's not...

Here's why...

- *You* **don't** *need to write or record a sales letter - which can take* *forever* *(even for us)*

- *You* **don't** *have to build a complicated sales funnel*

- *It's uber-low-risk with virtually* **no or low** *overhead*

- *It's the fastest way to establish yourself as an expert or thought leader*

And

> *- It's the best way to* **build a list***.*

So there. :-)

This Wednesday, *I am going to interview Mike Koenigs all for YOU.*

I am going to pick Mike K's brain and get him to spill the beans on everything he knows about this new trend and how you can start using it right now – for any business, in any country or language in the world.

So you should be there. Here's the link =>

(You get the free book there, too.)

The live event is this Wednesday at 1pm PST and 4pm EST.

Best,
Name

PS - Mike Koenigs is also giving away a **free Apple Watch** *live and you could be the winner! Not only do you get to see the latest and greatest new money-making media, but you can also win something new and cool.*

Click Here to Register.

PPS - Why you need to be live?

What about "Replays?" We Knew you were going to ask.

When we send out a replay, it will may be edited with some key parts that are best demonstrated live. Plus, ONLY live attendees will also get Mike's slides from his presentation.

PPPS - After spending some time with Mike Koenigs, he shared the same presentation that you're going to see. And as we said... **we were blown away***...which is one more reason why you should be there live.*

II. The morning of the show: send a reminder

Subj: BIG Things Happen Today

Hey <name>,

(Your name) here again...

We feel that today's live event is VERY important.

In fact, I wanted to tell you the TOP 3 reasons why you should be there..

1. *Webcasts are quickly becoming THE single best way to engage your audience, create demand, and sell more stuff. This is using live interactive video – not old-fashioned webinars.*

2. *Webcast customers SPEND MORE, are more engaged, refund less, buy at a higher price, open more of your emails, click more often, are more engaged on social, and are more action and implementation oriented.*

3. *We're going to show you irrefutable proof that webcasts can work in every business (even yours) with live case studies, Q&A, and hot seats.*

BONUS: *You get Mike Koenigs' #1 best selling book "How to Be a Video Interview Pro" for free. In the book, you get the formula connecting, meeting and working with celebrities (he's interviewed people like Tony Robbins, Tim Ferriss, Paula Abdul, actor Richard Dreyfuss and many others).*

And yes, it will be a 100% LIVE EVENT with Q&A, giveaways and FUN!

This LIVE event will be held TODAY, Wednesday, June 1st at 4:00 pm EST

You can reserve your seat HERE.

Oh btw, we've already got XXXX people registered (as you've probably already guessed) ... so if you signed up before.. SHOW UP EARLY and SAY HI IN CHAT (before we get full).

See you there,
Name

III. When the show goes live: send a "We're LIVE" email

Subject: [We're LIVE!] Come and join us right now...

We're live RIGHT NOW.

Go here to get on our LIVE webcast on the single most-important emerging technology - webcasts!

Hop on the event to hang out with us and be sure to grab a pen and paper. We'll show you step-by-step how to launch and profit from live interactive video.

[image]

It all happens NOW!

We'll also take your questions live!

All you have to do is join us here now.

Talk to you in a few,
Name

PS - Someone is about to win an Apple Watch. Will it be YOU?

Join us to find out.

PPS.- don't forget - webcast customers refund less, buy at a higher price, open more of your emails, click more often, are more engaged on social, and are generally more action oriented. You'll see why...and you also get the step-by-step formula for webcasts - even if you hate the way you look on camera.

IV. The afternoon (or day after) the show: send a replay link and/or reminder of the offer

Subj: How to make $212 per attendee
Subj: DEADLINE tonight
Subj: This goes "poof" tonight…
Subj: Going, going, gone!

Tick-tock, tick-tock…

Mike Koenigs' definitive Webcast Profit Toolkit goes away tonight at midnight.

That means you have just a few hours to grab the same system that fueled 12 (count 'em) 7-figure launches.

You get the picks and the shovels, but also the treasure maps to the most successful webcasts on the planet.

YHis most recent program earned $212 per attendee – and he'll give you the exact presentation and system he used to make that happen.

You'll get step--by-step resources including all the sales copy you need. All you have to do is fill in a few blanks and you're done. We'll give you all the webpages, emails, and social media posts you need to build a raving group of webcast fans.

But you have to grab it now.

(This closes tonight at Midnight)

Go get yours now.

Best,
Name

PS - This is the same system that's been used to earn millions of dollars in online sales for years, and by NY Times #1 Bestselling Authors, JJ Virgin, John Assaraf and other super smart business people who see the writing

2. Affiliate Partners (aka—someone else's customers)

A great supplement to your list is someone else's list! Who A great supplement to your list is someone else's list! Who else do you know or follow or work with who has a following or network of people who would find value in your webcast? It could be colleagues, it could even be competitors. Think about it, by providing value to their people, you're making your affiliates look good (not to mention you can offer them a cut of the profit for the products you sell to their viewers.)

Affiliate partnerships are a fast and easy way to gain followers and build your reputation in your industry. Reach out to some influencers, get their followers online, and your profits will increase significantly.

This is a copy of the exact email I send to my affiliate partners to get them interested in promoting one of my products.

Subject: *Enclosed - a check for $75,994.00 written to YOU 4 days after completing a webcast*

Hi [name],

Below are the results from a webcast I did with Mike Filsaime on June 7th - 160 sales @ $1997.00 each.

Four days later, I cut them a check for $75,994.00 for the first part of their commission.

The deal is simple - watch this short under 2 minute video from Mike Filsaime describing what happened: https://youtu.be/NvG4Z-wBuhc

As Mike said in the video, this is the highest converting webcast they've ever done - here are the results at 160 sales with click conversions at $100.38 with a $173.94 per attendee value. We finished at 160 total and have a total of 12 refunds, single-digits which is very good for a high-priced product like this.

Clicks from Email Promo	Total Registrants	Live Attendees	Clicks on Buy Link	Total Sales	
9,378	3,875	1,837	3,183		
				Units Sold	160
				Price	$1,997
Earnings Per Click	Earnings Per Registrant	Earnings Per Attendee	Click Value Conversion	Total Sales	$319,520
$34.07	$82.46	$173.94	$100.38		

The replay of the webcast is available here:
www.WebcastProfitToolkit.com

We just completed another webcast with Jason Fladlien - to a small audience and here are his results so far:

Total Sales: $56,600

Earnings Per Registrant: $49.37

Earnings Per Attendee: $233.33

Here's a replay of the webcast: [LINK HERE]

Would you like to schedule a similar webcast with your audience so that you can get a big check like this?

It's easy and you don't have to do anything except send a series of emails already written for you to your list. It's literally plug-in and make money. We also have a free gift for everyone who registers, which is my latest bestselling book, "How to Be a Video Interview Pro". Books regularly help the registration conversions exceed 50% and as high as 72%.

Everything is turnkey, done for you and we'll FedEx or Wire Transfer 80% of your first month's commissions within 5 business days of completing the promotion directly to you.

Mike Koenigs

PS - To schedule a webcast with your audience, reply to both myself and my assistant who is cc'd above.

3. Interviews—Borrowed Credibility

There are two ways to use interviews to your promotion advantage:

First, *offer to be interviewed*. Influencers are always looking for new and interesting content. In the weeks leading up to your webcast, reach out to influencers in your industry and ask if they would like to interview you! And in the interview, talk about your upcoming webcast event.

Second, *interview others*. Conduct interviews with experts in your industry that will be included in the webcast. Then, as you are promoting your webcast, advertise that so-and-so expert will be on the line to discuss XYZ. I call this "borrowing credibility." When you interview someone, they are essentially loaning you their credibility. Even if people don't know you, if they know your expert, you gain instant cred by association.

Someone who has done an incredible job of this is Tim Ferriss. You might remember Tim as the author of the New York Times Bestseller *The 4-Hour Work Week*. His current podcast is phenomenal and he has access to just about anyone. He recently did an interview with Arnold Schwarzenegger which gave him access to all of Hollywood. Now, Tim's been at it for a while—but he is walking proof that borrowed credibility can get you the keys to virtually any kingdom you choose and unlimited promotional power.

4. Speaking
Every speaking opportunity is an opportunity to build and grow an audience and promote your webcast. In the days and weeks leading up to your event, if there are live physical stages you can stand on, do it! Be sure you collect email addresses from the audience and then send them announcements about your upcoming webcast.

Not only is speaking a great opportunity to spread the word about your webcast, it will make you a better webcaster. Learning how to build energy, learning how to present, read an audience and learning body language… these are all essential skills and every time you speak for an audience is an opportunity to get better

5. Books—Amazon Author Page—Event Page
Did you know that Amazon Author pages get extremely high rankings in search engines? And once you have an Author page, you can create an Event Page. Then, anytime you have a webcast

or a speaking event of any kind of a promotion, you can actually add that to you Amazon calendar. What better way to promote your event than to link to your highly-search-optimized Author page.

6. Webcast Workshops, Interviews and Podcasts
One of the best ways to build an audience is by borrowing credibility and authority. This is best done by inviting an expert to interview on a show and asking them to post details to their social media, or ideally, promote it to their audience or list.

Another great way to build a list or grow your visibility, authority and value is to offer to be an expert on a podcast. Just search on iTunes podcasts for topics that are relevant to your area of expertise and send an email and social post to the owner of that podcast with a brief description of what you can speak about, what you have to share, a high-value takeaway you can give their audience.

The most important part about this strategy is you need to establish rapport by providing some information that proves you know their audience and understand their platform. The easiest way to do this is listen to or watch several of their podcast episodes, read their blogs, follow them on social channels and reference specific things you like about their content and can add more value.

7. Social Media Promotions
Of course you should get super social about your webcast. In addition to posting your event on social pages, Facebook, Google+, Twitter, InstaGram, Pinterest, LinkedIn and any other sites, here are some free websites that promote webcasts:

www.WebinarBase.com
www.WebinarListings.com
www.EventBrite.com
www.SlideShare.com
www.Tumblr.com

Two places that give you a huge boost in search engine listings are creating free Facebook and Google Hangouts events.

If you have an Amazon Author Page, you can post physical or virtual events on those pages free of charge. That way you're getting the credibility and authority boosting power of Amazon behind you.

And don't forget the power of your own personal email list. Whenever you have a webcast planned, add a link to your email schedule and ask people to forward the event opportunity to people on their list too.

8. Paid traffic
This is one of the great advantages of webcasting over infomercials or traditional media—highly targeted messaging. If you know the demographics of your Market, who they follow and what they're interested in, you can get on Facebook and send ads about your webcast to a highly targeted audience for a very reasonable price. Never in the history of promotion and advertising has it ever been so cheap and so easy to get in touch with your specific audience.

Paid Facebook ads, retargeting, ads on YouTube—when done right, these are all high-return investments.

Remember: Market - Message – Medium.

9. Traditional Media
If you're trained, and I think the training is worth it, getting exposure on traditional media including radio, television, newspapers and magazines can also work for promoting your webcast. Truthfully, the days when exposure on television meant a bump in sales are over. The good news is television and other traditional media outlets still equals powerful credibility and authority. So if you can get on TV or radio or in the newspaper... go for it. Build your credibility, talk about your webcast, gain followers, increase sales at the live webcast event. You'll also benefit from building a media "sizzle reel" which will help you get and stay in the news. Exposure builds momentum and more exposure!

10. iTunes, Audible and Amazon Audio
Your video webcasts can be easily saved and repurposed as audio files and distributed as video and audio podcasts or even

audio books. Think of all the people who walk around with headphones. They never take them out! Which means they're always listening to something. Shouldn't they be listening to you?

Capturing Leads, Maximizing Content

Here is the final step to effective promotion of your webcast. Lead Capture.

The final step in promoting your webcast building a database of email addresses. It doesn't matter how much content you create or where you put it—if you don't have an email address to send the webcast invite to, your promotional strategy is about as effective as tying a note to a balloon and hoping it lands in someone's yard who cares.

Social media followers aren't enough. I've known celebrities with over 400,000 followers on Facebook, Twitter, Instagram and Pinterest who can't get 300 people to show up to a webcast.

We're going to get a little technical here, but only a little. To get an audience to show up, you need to invite them to register their name and email address on a lead capture page and send them a reminder email.

We use lead capture and autoresponder systems and tools including:

- LeadPages.net
- ClickFunnels
- Aweber
- InfusionSoft
- WebinarJam
- Instant Customer (now known as TPNI Engage)

There are hundreds of other services for making lead capture pages... (just search for "lead capture page" in Google).

Here are some examples of some very successful "lead capture" pages we use:

THE ULTIMATE BUSINESS BRANDING & POSITIONING TOOL

Click The Download Button Below for Instant Access To
The "Publish & Profit" Book & Video Series

DOWNLOAD NOW

Download Your Book Now!

Statistically 59%-74% of the visitors who reach this page click the button and fill out a form to get a free book and register to watch the videos.

This is another example of a very high-converting lead capture page:

The TRUTH About Sugar

Inflammation, Fatigue, Heart Disease, Obesity… and CRAVING IT!

FEATURING **JJ VIRGIN**

LIVE WEBCAST ON HOW TO DISCOVER THE HIDDEN SUGARS THAT ARE MAKING YOU SICK (and FAT)

**Wednesday, June 17th
5pm PST | 8pm EST**

Replay Provided To Registrants, Register Now For Live Webcast.

- 3 Time New York Times Best Selling Author
- Celebrity Nutrition & Fitness Expert
- What's the HIDDEN enemy in your house, and what can you do about it? Find out from me personally
- Save your seat at my no-cost Powerful Free Webinar on SUGAR

Enter your first name

Enter your email address

REGISTER NOW

🔒 Your information entered here is secure and will never be sold, rented, or used for third-party commercial purposes.

Mark Hyman, MD, *Author of the #1 New York Times bestseller The Blood Sugar Solution; The 10 Day Detox Diet*

Opens your eyes to how much sugar you're really eating, and provides an actionable plan to cut down on the sweet stuff and feel better fast.

Sara Gottfried, MD, *Harvard-trained MD with 20+ years of experience and the author of the bestselling book, The Hormone Cure*

JJ provides a step-by-step strategy to gradually remove sugar. If you want to ditch stubborn belly fat and look 10 years younger, you need this!

704% of the visitors who reach this page click the button and fill out a form to watch the webcast with JJ Virgin and Mike Koenigs.

On the day of the webcast, an email message gets sent to the registrants with a link to a page that looks like this:

This is your "tool" that displays your video, allows the viewers to share the page with other people who might show up to watch you, a way to chat with you and ask questions or make comments and the all-important BUY BUTTON.

This page can be built by anyone who has basic HTML experience.

Ready, Set, Go!

It's time. Tell the world about your webcast. Start creating content—make a few minutes every day to come up with a "riff". Make a free report. Create a podcast. Write an article. Then get your info out there—send it to your followers, get other experts on board, pay Facebook to spread the word to a highly targeted market. Finally, capture the emails (gold!) so you can send them the opt-in and they can join you LIVE!

hich is the next step… now that you're going to have people there… how exactly do you perform a webcast? Even if you have no speaking experience, even if you hate how your nose looks on camera, I'm going to teach you the keys to performing the perfect webcast (even if it isn't perfect!).

Chapter 5:
Step Four - Perform

• •

"Don't let the fear of striking out hold you back."

Babe Ruth

• •

CASE STUDY: ANDY Lockwood — The Man Who Faced the Camera (even though he was nervous as hell!)

I recently had an expert in my studio named Andy. Andy has a very creative approach to helping parents send their kids to private schools - most of them aren't affordable for these families. He teaches a system and provides consulting services to qualify for grants or get substantial discounts legally and ethically.

He's always looking for better ways to grow his audience and expertise and started using webcasts to teach and sell.

We recently started a program that we call the "You Everywhere Now LIVE! Bootcamp" to teach entrepreneurs how to present and perform on camera and star on a show with other business owners that broadcasts live to our audience, gets distributed via a podcast and turned into a book on Amazon.

We invited and trained 8 different blockbuster entrepreneurs to share their wisdom on a show.

Unfortunately, for nearly all eight of them, it was their first time on camera in a real studio. No amount of visualizing their viewers in their underwear were going to calm these nerves. So the day before the webcast, I walked them all through the steps I'm about to teach you now.

The next morning, it was lights, camera, action and no one passed out! In fact, they successfully generated leads and earned several thousand dollars while the broadcast was running.

Here's a picture of us as we celebrated the completion of the "You Everywhere Now LIVE!" show together:

And here's Andy Lockwood as he confidently presents to an audience of hundreds of people from all over the world including the United States, Canada, Australia, France, Germany, Switzerland, China and even Kenya!

Presenting confidently on camera is a learnable skill that anyone can master...it just takes a little bit of confidence and courage to get started and a willingness to feel a bit comfortable the first time.

You can watch several recordings of Andy and seven other entrepreneurs who took a chance to join me for a day in our studio to present and perform on a live webcast for the "Webcast Profit Toolkit Bootcamp LIVE!" - the podcast and recording can be found right here: www.MiXiV.com/yenlive

There is a lot to think about when putting a webcast together. You're about to read a decade's worth of experience in a list of 25 easy strategies. When it comes to webcasting, small things make a big difference. If you want someone to value you or your brand or your knowledge or the product you're selling them—or if like me, you want to make a million bucks—you've gotta look like a million bucks on camera! This chapter ensures you'll look like a pro every time.

You can get a full book with illustrations at www.VideoInterview Book.com and a handy infographic that will make sure every webcast you do (especially if it includes remote interviews) looks and sounds absolutely fantastic.

Strategy #1: Position Your Camera Lens Above Eye Level

Let me ask you two questions…

1. Would you like to lose 10 pounds instantly?
2. Would you consider it rude if someone you were speaking to insisted you looked straight up their nose?

Hopefully the answer to both of those questions was *YES!*

The most common (huge) mistake I see people make is they do video interviews with their cameras below eye level. The result is they look fat, hunched over and old. Worse? The person on the other end winds up counting nose hairs—if they're lucky.

Have you ever watched a bridal party getting their photos taken? Where is the photographer typically standing? Up on top of a bench, or a retaining wall, or hanging from a tree—anything to get above eye level of the subjects. It's the instant diet all brides (and grooms) love because they'll look 10 pounds lighter.

This simple shift of the lens will shave pounds, years and mean you don't have to worry about shaving your nose hairs.

Here's the rule: Position your camera lens approximately 1-3 inches (2-6 cm) ABOVE your eyes. If you're using a laptop, just put IT on top of a stack of books or anything that puts it above eye level. If you're using a professional camera or webcam, adjust accordingly. And, if you do use a stack of books or something, make sure the computer is stable so it doesn't wiggle around or move when you're speaking. Not even a little bit. A shaky or moving lens is amateurish and very annoying to the viewer on the other end.

Strategy #2: Look at the Lens, Not the Screen!

A very close second to the up-the-nose mistake is this one; amateurs who *think* they're talking to the camera but in reality, all the viewer sees is a buffoon staring off into a distant corner of the screen.

This is a *huge* problem. Not only does it scream rookie, but when someone isn't making eye contact (and in video, you make eye contact with your viewers by looking directly at the camera lens) they appear disconnected, sketchy or just plain creepy. These are not the thoughts you want running through your viewers' minds as they watch your webcast while you do your best to develop trust and rapport.

At first, looking at a tiny lens on a webcam feels a lot less natural than looking at a human on a screen but this is one of those subtle skills that separate a pro from an amateur.

So here's how it's done: Identify your webcam. Got it? Good. Now look at it. The *whole* time. Never stop looking at the webcam. Don't take your eyes off it. Congrats. You'll be better at webcasting than 70% of the others who try with that one strategy right there.

Strategy #3: "Frame" Your Shot

The best shots are well-framed. No one cares what you're saying if they can't see you saying it! After you've set your camera above eye-level and you're sure sure you're looking at the lens, the next step is to properly position yourself on the screen.

Here are a few rules of thumb:

Make sure you have some headroom at the top of the shot. We should be able to see the top of your head and a little empty space above it - but don't center your eyes right in the middle of the screen.

Don't cut off any piece of your face or head. I don't care if you have the biggest face in the east, I want to see every last beautiful inch of it!

Also, I often put an LCD monitor on a stand next to me in the shot and then show my slides as I speak so they're in the background as well. These are all great ways to reinforce a brand, and it looks really professional too. Lastly, if you don't have a much of a background, make sure your head is close to the top of the frame and use a neutral or simple color. There's nothing wrong with a solid white background (like the old Apple commercials).

Strategy #4: Backlighting is for Horror Movies!

Speaking of backgrounds... when choosing a background for your interview, remember this: backlights are for horror movies ONLY. Unless you are Alfred Hitchcock and about to be attacked by a demonic flock of birds, make sure you are not setting up your camera facing a window or a bright light. The bright light needs to be on your face, not behind you.

Strategy #5: Light from the Front

So naturally, if Strategy #4 is to not have a light behind you, it would make sense that Strategy #5 is having a light in *front of you*. Go straight to Amazon — you'll be able to get really nice, affordable LED lights that will make you look like a million bucks. Search "web cam lights" and you'll find a variety of great options.

Depending on the strength and type light, you should place it approximately 2-3 feet away from your face. The only trick is, you don't want to be *overlit*. You just need good quality lighting that fills up your face without creating glare. And take a close look at yourself to make sure there aren't any big shadows anywhere— sometimes something as simple as a curl in your hair can block the light from your eye or cast a shadow across your cheek.

Strategy #6: Neat, Uncluttered Background

Make sure you have an interesting but uncluttered background. I've seen interviews with people who are supposed to be successful and wealthy, and it looks like they live in a dumpster because there's disarray, stacks of junk and garbage behind them.

If you're in front of a door, close it. Or better yet, make sure your camera is facing a background that will be interesting, attractive and relevant to your audience. Make sure whatever you are in front of is *brand representative*. Get your pets outta there, too. There is nothing more distracting in a webcast than a cat strolling around "on set."

Strategy #7: Smile! :)

This one is easy and easily missed. SMILE!

Smiling is FREE! Smiling not only creates happy chemicals inside *your* brain, but people connect and relate to you. In many, many studies that have been conducted on television personalities, the ones who smile the most are liked the most, they're trusted the most and, I would venture to guess, they make the most money.

I tell you to smile (something that seems obvious) because truthfully, if it's just you and a webcam, it might seem strange at first. After all, you're technically talking to a lens on a camera. What about that inspires smiling? It might seem forced or fake, but trust me when I say, the faster you can get over *that*, the faster you'll connect with your viewers. No one wants to buy from Eeyore (the sad donkey in *Winnie the Pooh*), and really, no one wants to *listen* to Eeyore either. Put a smile on your face to create a smile in your voice. It doesn't cost a nickel to smile and the more you do it, the more natural it becomes.

Strategy #8: Control the Noise

Babies. I get it. They cry. They giggle. They need stuff. That's fine... just not within earshot of the mic. Same with pets. We already talked about cats wandering in the background, but if you've got a yappy puppy, though I'm sure he's super cute, barking dogs are not cute during a webcast unless it's a webcast about dogs. Even worse? You hopping up to say, "Oh, just a second. I've got to run away and put my dog away." If you do that, you'll lose your audience. They'll be asking themselves, "Who is this clown?" It completely degrades the experience and the confidence and trust someone has to have in you. If you can't control your environment, how can you expect your audience to believe you can control and provide good value either? You will be judged by this.

That being said, there are other "less obvious" noise culprits that, unless you're an audio engineer, you probably wouldn't even notice them... but your audience will.

Body noise. These are the noises you unconsciously make—like sniffling, snorting, hard breathing, throat-clearing and jewelry.

Room and ambient noise. When you walk into a room, pay attention to subtle whirring or buzzing. Do you have fans that are turning on and off all the time? Air conditioning? A hum from a washing machine on the other side of the wall? Is your computer noisy? How about your chair? Pay attention to the sounds in your environment.

Others include banging on a desk or table surface as you speak, bumping the microphone with your gestures (and hair for women), typing on the keyboard, folks who wear loose jewelry including bracelets, watches, necklaces or earrings that clink and clang. If it's noisy or can rattle, ring, bang or clank, take it off.

Luckily, there is a quick tip for preventing some ugly sounding noise when you're doing webcasts; set up your microphone with some pillows surrounding it so it doesn't reverberate and bounce. It actually deadens the sound.

When it comes to webcasting, you don't have the luxury of fixing audio problems in post-production, because you're *LIVE*. It's important to do everything you can to eliminate the sources of noise in the first place before you record.

Strategy #9: Wrap Your Package

You get one first impression, so don't blow it by looking like a slob. I say "Wrap the Package" and that package is *you!*

Dress for success. Dress for results. Dress for the income you want, not the income you have. People will judge you based on how you present yourself. Unless you're in the garbage business, don't dress in garbage. Put on a nice shirt. Take care of your hair. Brush your teeth for gosh sakes. Look good. If you're a woman, make sure your dress, makeup and accessories are what I call "brand representative". If you're a man, don't be a schlub. Okay?

And if you're whining, "I don't know how to dress," or "I don't know what to wear" or "I don't have anything to wear," then go get someone to dress you. Seriously, if you haven't done this before, I highly recommend you actually go to a client-focused department store like Nordstroms, and ask for someone to help you pick out clothing that match your skin tone, brand, and line of work. It's worth the investment.

My dad used to tell me, "You act the way you dress." As a kid, I didn't like hearing that and really didn't believe it until I hired someone to dress me for the first time. It totally changed how people recognized and even treated me. The first time I wore an ensemble chosen by a professional was the first time, in my entire *life*, I've ever gotten a compliment on my clothing. I mean, I'm from a small town in Minnesota; not really the fashion metropolis of the world...

Last tip: make sure you wear solid colors; never wear plaids or checkerboard patterns because they'll create "moire" patterns on video. And if you ever wear a lavalier microphone, you should wear a button-up shirt so it can be easily attached and not get bumped or rubbed by clothing or jewelry.

Strategy #10: Create a Memorable Theme

Strategy number ten is to have a theme. In addition to looking good and your first impression, you've got to get and keep your audience's attention by being unique and interesting. Most people decide whether or not they're going to keep watching you in 4-8 seconds. Your goal is to get them to stick around for at least 30 seconds so you can get to the "what's in it for them" part of the interview.

Maybe it's a costume, or a spiel, or a wacky hook. Why? Because if your webcast is yawn-city, even if there *is* valuable content, no one learns anything because they can't stay awake long enough to watch it (and they *certainly* won't stay around to buy anything).

If you have just a little theme that represents what you're going to be talking about—something you can act out—you will stand out among the hundreds of others who were not brave enough to do it.

Your success depends on whether or not you can get and keep people's attention. A memorable theme is an easy way to do it. It could be the background. It could be a costume that you open up with, or some sort of a tchotchke, but having a theme for an interview means you will be memorable.

Strategy #11: Use Props

Right there with creating a memorable theme is using props! Get, use and talk about props. Use them as metaphors for your presentation, speech or sales strategy. It's a fun way to liven things up, to keep people's attention and to keep them guessing—what the heck is this person gonna do next?? Especially in webcasting, being able to talk about a prop—holding them, holding them up to the camera—it creates a depth of visual interest. Now they're not just interested in you, but in your topic, the interview itself and the way you're presenting the material.

And! If you simply *mention or motion* to the prop at the beginning of the webcast and say something like, "More about that later…" you'll "open loops" for your viewers—that's an NLP or "Neuro

Linguistic Programming" term. Humans always want to feel as though we've reached a state of completion. Therefore, if someone sees a prop and you say, "In a moment we're going to talk about this diddly-doo and why it's important", they'll likely stick around to find out what that diddly-doo is and what it does.

Props are also excellent metaphors—when you can illustrate a complex idea or subject with a visually-interesting prop, you'll have a higher likelihood of being able to communicate your ideas in a way that appeals to every type of learning style.

Props = good for webcasting!

Strategy #12: Prepare a Bio and Curiosity Statement

Every time you start a show, you need to assume the audience might be meeting you for the first time. Assume nothing. So it's important that you have a quick description of who you are, what you do, who you do it for in a way that hooks the viewer, relays value, trust and creates enough interest that they want to stick around to see what you have to offer.

Here's an example:

"Hi, my name is Mike Koenigs, 8-time #1 bestselling author, cancer survivor and creator of Publish and Profit and the Webcast Profit Toolkit. Stick around because today you're going to find out how to turn your ideas into highly engaging, profitable live video events so that you can share your message, grow an audience and make money from the comfort of your home or office without having to travel, even if you're non-technical or afraid of talking to a camera."

When you register to get the free Video Interview Book, you'll receive a copy of my full bio that you can model for your own webcasts.

Strategy #13: Open with a Story

Remember how I opened this book? With a story—the story of when I made a million dollars. Now, I didn't tell you that story just for fun, and I certainly didn't tell it to brag...

No, I told you a story because sharing a personal story is the easiest way to win over an audience in less than a minute. Open up your webcast with a compelling story. Make your opening sentence, "Let me tell you a story…" The human brain is programmed to respond and listen to stories—it's how we learn. They won't be able to resist you.

Have a story that's relevant, that is germane to the theme, and ties in your bio and the topic being discussed.

Strategy #14: Keep Your Hands Under Control

This may seem trivial but let me ask you, how do you feel when someone pokes you? Or points at your face? Or waves their fingers within inches of your eyes?

Not good, right?

That's what you're doing if you point directly at the camera. Because the distance between the viewer and their screen is usually a short one, when you point a finger at them, your finger is only three inches from their face!

Another gesture to avoid: finger templing. Never temple your fingers. This is a subconscious or overt sign of superiority from the speaker's perspective that's saying "I'm better or smarter than you." Politicians do this when they're speaking to someone they don't respect. There's a natural reaction most people have to "reel away" from this posture. As a result, it breaks intimacy, trust and connection with your audience.

These are subtle mistakes, but when you commit *hand-crimes*, your viewers sense the barriers they create. They sense the "I am better than you" undertone. We notice and feel it. It feels wrong. It's like putting up a concrete barrier between the connection we have with each other.

Use open gestures. Arms that are inviting. Think big, warm, virtual hugs. Don't put up hand barriers. Don't poke at people. It's just not nice.

Strategy #15: Fifteen Minute Rule

The Fifteen Minute Rule is simple: 15 minutes before your webcast, get prepared. Run through everything you want to accomplish and do in your webcast in your head. Look over the showflow again. Drink a big glass of water. Get your props setup and next to you. Get your butt in place. Think about your theme. Think about the story you're going to open with. Start smiling. Imagine how you're going to make the viewer smile, laugh, cry or feel.

If you can get prepared a half an hour before, even better.

Certainly, things go wrong during live events—it comes with the territory. But there's no reason for mistakes that could have been prevented with a quick 15 minute review.

Strategy #16: Restart Your Computer!

Put this at the top of the 15 minute list. Make sure you restart your computer and all your equipment! Shortly before the interview, shutdown and restart.

Computers have a nasty reputation of crashing at inopportune times, especially if they've been running for days or weeks without a break.

Chances are, you're likely running a bunch of apps you don't even know you're running. Web browsers are notorious for being giant memory hogs and cause "leaks" that wind up slowing down your computer which can affect your webcast.

Restart. Clean the slate. The last thing you need is for your computer to freeze up when you're in the middle of an emotionally-charged story and after you've built a great connection with the audience.

Strategy #17: Test Your Connection Speed

If you are one of those people who are still living (if that's what you call living) with slow internet, stop right now and upgrade your internet speed to the fastest you can afford *immediately*. Fast connections will always make you more money than you spend.

If you're working with a slow internet connection, there's a high probability your audio is going to sound horrible, your video is going to look unprofessional, if it's viewable at all. There are speed tests available online—all you gotta do is go to Google and search for 'Internet speed test'. Check your connection speed.

One other tip: Whenever possible, connect your computer directly to your router with a cable. It's sad but Wifi is not live video's friend. It can be degraded by interference, mirrors or microwaves.

Strategy #18: Turn Off File Sharing

Filesharing on a home or office network shows down your internet connection and can make your audio or video sound or look horrible. Turn it off.

Still not clear what that means? Make sure your computer and every computer on your network are not downloading files while you're doing a webcast. If you're on a shared connection, let everyone know when you're about to do a webcast so they can stop the downloads until after you're done.

Strategy #19: No Uploads

Uploads are one of the biggest enemies of any audio or video interview. In fact, they're worse than downloads. Once you've restarted your computer and made sure nobody is sharing files on your network, make sure you keep all unnecessary applications turned off. Even a web browser is a potential liability for causing audio or video glitches to occur.

BitTorrent sharing, FTP uploads, automatic backup operations, extra apps, clicks or actions can affect your sound or your video quality.

Most internet connections have much slower upload than download speeds. And for you, the upload speed is actually MORE important than download speeds. So anything that is hogging your connection can harm the quality of your recording stream.

Strategy #20: In-Ear Monitor

High-quality webcasts do involve investing in some equipment. Fortunately, the equipment is minimal and available without spending a small fortune. The of the first pieces of equipment you'll need is an in-ear-monitor. Now, I know what you might be thinking, "Mike, an in-ear-monitor is more expensive! Can't I just get a pair of headphones and get the same result?"

In terms of sound, probably. In terms of look, branding, and customer perception... an in-ear monitor will give you a much better look. Remember, you're on camera. You don't want cords hanging off your face or a big clunky headset messing up your hair. If you want to look like a respectable, branded professional AND record a webcast that's television-worthy you've got to get an in-ear monitor. There's just no way around it.

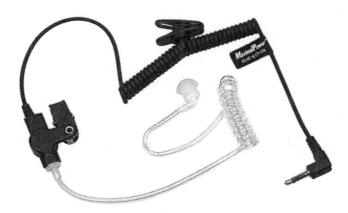

You can get an inexpensive in-ear monitor for as little as $10 on Amazon that fits in your ear and isn't visible while you talk. This is the same type of thing that a security guard wears - make sure it has a 3.5mm headphone jack!

There are a lot of different models—the cheapest ones are as low as $10 and the super fancy ones can go over $1,000. The simple ones are the same headsets you see security guards wearing. You'll need an extension cable for it, but just plug them into your computer jack, clip it into your ears, snaps on to the back of your shirt and wah-la! Super pro vs. super dork.

What's important is, *remember*, you are there to put on a good show and to *look good*, so you're packaging and your presentation is important. Unless you live in your grandmother's basement and you live on PB&J sandwiches, I'd recommend investing in an in-ear monitor that serves you and your brand.

Strategy #21: High-Quality Microphone

While we're talking about equipment, a good microphone will cost you less than $100 while a bad microphone (aka: the one currently built into your computer) will cost you *thousands* in sales and potentially *millions* in lost opportunities. A bad microphone creates a significantly lower quality recording. I recommend checking out either a Blue Nessie, which costs about $70 on Amazon, or a Blue Yeti. They cost around $100. The Blue Nessie sounds great and connects seamlessly with an in-ear monitor with a built-in connector.

To make buying a microphone and other equipment painless, I've included a link to my free "Interviewer Gear Guide" when you respond to the "Call to Action" box below.

Strategy #22: Get a High-Quality Webcam or Camera

The built-in camera that comes with most computers and laptops these days is *pretty good*. However, if you *can*, you might as well get the top of the line. The hottest camera right now, as we write this book, is the Logitech webcam — the C930e. This thing looks awesome, and if it's lit properly, most people can't tell that it isn't a $2,000 professional camera—and the Logitech only costs about $100 or so.

To get the next level in quality, you need to connect a camcorder ($300 and up) and get a computer interface that costs between $150-$300. That option does give you a noticeable improvement in quality but it's a significant jump in cost and not necessary.

Strategy #23: Record and Edit the Webcast for Encore Presentations

When you broadcast your webcast with Google Hangouts, YouTube Live, LiveStream or uStream, you're already and automatically backing up your show so that it can be edited later.

If you use more advanced software for producing your webcasts such as Wirecast or a NewTek Tricaster, those systems can record a local copy of your webcast directly to your hard drive. This is normally much higher quality than what is being saved and stored on Hangouts or YouTube.

The show can then be edited with ScreenFlow, Camtasia, iMovie, Final Cut Pro, Premiere, Sony Vegas or whichever video editing software you or your editor prefers.

The reason you might want to do this is because you may want to remove some mistakes, specific day or time references, awkward moments or rearrange a segment to streamline a program.

Strategy #24: No Sound Effects

First, let me ask you this: How do you feel when you have a guest over for dinner who looks at their phone all evening? How would you like it if they took calls in the middle of dinner and left every message notification on so you could hear every text message and email as it came in? Would that make you feel important and prioritized? Would it make your dinner intimate and connected?

No. Of course not.

Even though this should be obvious, in this phone-obsessed world we live it I feel I must explicitly say: Do your viewers a favor and PUT THE PHONE DOWN! Turn off your computer sounds, phone and other noisemakers while you do your webcast. Especially Skype notifications. Dings, dongs, bings, woots, buzzes and boops make you appear very unprofessional and amateurish.

Strategy #25: Interact with the Audience!

It may be last on this list but as far as I'm concerned this is *the most important element of a kick butt webcast*. Remember, one of the three major components of a webcast is the interactive chat; the window to the side of the screen where your audience can interact with you and with the other viewers.

It is through this chatting that you are able to read your potential customers' minds—you can read their questions and adjust your message. You can identify what's really resonating and give them more of it.

The chat is what gives live webcasting the unstoppable, insurmountable cutting-edge. But here's the catch. It only works if you *work it*. The interaction likely won't happen just on its own—you'll have to encourage it. You'll have to move it along.

The interactive strategy happens in three steps: Call for the interaction, watch the response, acknowledge the participants. For example: I often say throughout my webcasts, "If you're ready to take your financial future to the next level type 'Show me the money' in the chat right now!" I watch the viewers respond and the chat window flood with various versions of "show me the money," and then I *acknowledge* a few of them when they do. "Susan is ready to go to the next level, Steve is ready to see the money."

This recognition encourages them to participate more (and answers that ever-nagging question they might have—is this really live?). Eventually, after doing several webcasts, your audience will start to recognize each other, relationships form, and your shows become a fun place to hang out. These are all very good things.

An added benefit of encouraging interaction: you conquer distraction. One of the biggest challenges of a webcast is keeping the attention of your viewers. By constantly keeping their fingers busy in chat, you lessen their ability to keep busy elsewhere (texting, tweeting, twiddling). Encourage them to "write this down" or "enter their answer in chat," keep them busy and you'll keep their attention.

Here are the things we include that create desire and make people want to buy:

1. An introduction – welcome the viewer

2. Ask them to introduce themselves in the chat

3. Tell them what they're going to learn or experience during the show

4. Explain the big benefits – and the opportunity (lose weight, make money, start a business, feel better, look sexy, get smarter, save more)

5. Demonstrate the product

6. Show before and after pictures or videos

7. Interview successful customers or clients for social proof

8. Interview experts or authorities who boost your credibility

9. Answer questions

10. Ask for the sale (next chapter)!

Now, let's head straight to *Step Five, Profit!*

LET ME GUIDE YOU THROUGH A SALES WEBCAST

I'd love to show you step-by-step how a real sales webcast is presented so that you can model it for your own business. You'll have a chance to see a high-quality production using the strategies and techniques you're reading about right now in this book.

Register right now at www.WebcastProfitToolkit.com

Chapter 6: Step Five - Profit!

. . . .

"You don't close a sale; you open a relationship if you want to build a long-term successful enterprise."

Patricia Fripp

. . . .

The biggest psychological principle that you need to remember all the time when you are webcasting is asking for the sale if that's the point of your show.

Why is this so important?

Simple: the purpose of your webcast should be to inspire someone to take action - and usually that means buying your product, coaching, services, opportunity or consulting. At a minimum, it's asking them to IMPLEMENT.

Most people get timid and back out when it comes to asking for the sale.

Don't make that mistake.

Some of my best friends and clients first came to me because they bought one of my products on a webcast. The product changed their lives and businesses and they've come back over and over again since then.

Remember: a product is nothing more than a way to make money helping people. And you deserve to get paid for the help you provide.

When you get to the end of your presentation, you present your offer step-by-step and then tell people what to do next: visit a website, enter their credit card, fill out of qualification form or survey, call a phone number or send an email to get your program.

If you're using a system that allows you to "push" a sales button on screen, put it up and tell people to order.

Once you describe your guarantee and offer, answer questions in chat.

The recipe for success in a close is the following:

1. Transition to the close

2. "Future Pacing" also known as "The Ownership Experience" - describe what life will be like with your product

3. Walk through your offer

4. Describe your guarantee

5. Present your price

6. Include a deadline and scarcity

7. Add bonuses - which overcome buying objections

8. Answer questions

9. Review the offer again

10. Close the sale

Here's a description of each point, step-by-step:

Transition to the close
For example, you might say "with your permission, I'd like to share with you right now how we can work together".

Future Pacing
Next, we give our audience an opportunity to imagine what life would be like when they invest in and own your product.

So for example, I'll say something like this when I'm presenting my offer for the Webcast Profit Toolkit system:

"Now, imagine if I held you by the hand and guided you step by step through how to produce your own profitable webcast." Type "Yes" in chat if you can imagine yourself presenting on camera or if you would love to start your own show.

Now imagine if I brought you into my studio virtually from your home or office, or maybe right from your smartphone and I show you step by step how to make a product, I walked you through this entire process so that you could actually produce your first show, is that interesting to you?

Now, what if I gave you all the skills you need to be camera confident, so that you feel absolutely sure of yourself on camera? Type "Yes" in chat if you're not camera confident at all or want to be better - or even if you've never been on camera before. Perhaps you don't like the way you look, sound, or you've got some big story about how you're too old, too fat, have an accent, don't have the right kind of experience, expertise or whatever excuse has been standing in your way... What if I could erase those fears with you in about 15 minutes or less? What if I could give you or boost your on-camera charisma skills? Is that interesting to you?

What if I reviewed your product or offer? And if you don't have an offer, I gave you the tools and checklist and help you figure out what your offer should be and made it a no-brainer for your target audience to want to buy from you.

Imagine If I showed you how to pitch and sell on video, and helped you grow these skills so that you'd be able to take them with you for the rest of your life, and you learned the flow of a profitable webcast show.

What if I showed you step-by-step how you can use a webcast to make a product in a day or two that you could sell for $500, $1,000, $5,000 or even more? How valuable would that be to you right now?

Go ahead and type in how much additional income you feel you can make using webcasts in your business over the next year...

What if I gave you all the scripts and words you need so that you could persuade, influence and predict the buying behavior of your audience with integrity - and without sounding or being salesy.

And what if I gave you my technology, my tools, and my templates so you could simply copy and paste your webcast quickly and easily...in a few days or weeks from now or at whatever pace you're comfortable with?

Some of the tools I've used to make millions of dollars worth of income online with for myself and my clients and I know I can show you how to do it too - in just a few days of your time.

Walk through your offer

Now you'll show your "core offer" which is a list and description of everything the customer will receive when they purchase. It's important that you describe the BENEFITS of each item, not focus on features. The best way to remember to add a benefit is to use the transitional phrase **SO THAT YOU CAN**...

So for example, I might say, "The core training includes step-by-step training that guides you through how to do your own webcast" **SO THAT YOU CAN** *start presenting to your prospects or customers and make money in as little as 48 hours after you go through the initial training.*

Describe your guarantee

Generally, you'll include a no-questions-asked 30-day money back guarantee. Some advanced marketers include something like a "double your money back guarantee" when you implement and if you don't get results. That shows the audience you have confidence your product will work when they implement and get results.

The bottom line is you need to reverse the risk so that the customer feels confident they can try out your system and if it doesn't work for them for any reason, they don't feel like they're stuck.

Present your price

Present your price - and ideally, with one payment option. Note that there may be legal rules and guidelines in your state or country about how much you can charge for payments if they are higher than the single pay.

When you present your price, it makes sense to describe the value of each part or module of the program and compare it to what it would cost if it were purchased separately.

An example of this might be the value of the training if you worked 1:1 with someone could be $5,000 but the product may only cost $1,000.

Include a deadline and scarcity

As long as what you're saying is justifiable, verifiable and true, inserting a hard deadline and scarcity will motivate prospects to buy immediately.

The best example I can share with you would be the following:

"Our training begins this Monday at 10:00. The deadline for this offer is _Sunday at midnight_. When we re-launch this product, _it will cost $1,000 more_ and the training will not be happening live so you'll want to get in now. And as a special incentive for you to order right now, the next _20 people will receive a 30 minute 1:1 coaching call_ with me as soon as you complete module #1 but _only while we are doing this webcast_. Due to my schedule, I'm only able to accommodate a maximum of 20 people for the 1:1 calls and I normally charge $2,000 per call so it's like you're getting the product for free."

That statement included a hard deadline, a price increase and a scarcity offer. It's legitimate and real because training starts the next week, there's a limit to the amount of time you have available and you've justified the value of the call as a bonus.

Add bonuses - which overcome buying objections

Throughout the presentation, hopefully you've overcome buying objections by teaching and training and educating the audience. What I do is design bonuses that are added after I present the offer and price to overcome any objections someone might have and answer questions simultaneously.

Here are some bonuses I include with the Webcast Profit Toolkit:

- **How Look and Sound Great Every Time the Camera is on You!** This bonus overcomes the "I don't like the way I look or sound on camera" and "I have a face made for radio.

- **$100k in 100 Days : Mike's repeatable business success blueprint that's made over $1mm in less than 100 days 12 times in a row.** This bonus overcomes the "I don't have a business" and "How can I use this system to make money now?"

- **Grow Your List from Scratch: How to Build Effective Facebook Ad Campaigns to Generate Leads and Convert Them Into Sales.** This bonus overcomes the "I don't have a list", "Where am I going to get traffic?" and "How am I going to get people to sign up for my webcast?"

- **The Secret Countdown Video Formula that Sells For You: Three scripts valued over $10,000 each that have produced over $1,000,000 in sales you can model for your own programs.** This overcomes the common objection of "I don't know how to sell" or "I hate selling and I don't want to sound like a used car salesman"

Answer questions

Once you have gone through your offer and the bonuses, tell your audience to submit any questions they have and answer them. The MOST IMPORTANT lesson and recommendation I have is that you focus on answering questions that SELL YOUR PRODUCT. If you notice the same question being asked over and over again, make sure you clearly answer that question and if possible, mention a bonus you might have that overcomes that question or objection. Use lots of examples to illustrate what you mean in a way that is meaningful for the audience.

BONUS IDEA: I: If I see something show up over and over again and I know it is causing the prospect to not buy, I might invent a bonus ON THE SPOT that overcomes that objection, question or problem and offer to teach that in an upcoming training session. I've been able to create an additional $10,000-$20,000 or more in immediate sales with this single strategy.

Newbies have a tendency of indiscriminately answering every question that gets asked - even the ones asked by crazy people. THIS KILLS SALES. Focus on supporting the level-headed, high-quality questions, even if there's a nut in chat that repeats the same crazy-talk over and over again.

Remember that your chat is private property and this isn't a free-form place for "freedom of speech". After conducting hundreds of profitable webcasts, make sure you get rid of people who try to sell their products and services, become a distraction or are just plain dumb. Keep your eye on the prize and focus on interested prospects who are there to buy. Run a benevolent dictatorship, not a commune!

Review the offer again

Don't assume that the first time you went through your offer people understood what you were saying or followed everything in your close. There's a high probability they were looking at their email, chatting on the phone or paying attention to something else.

Go through your entire offer summary one more time and describe everything that's included. Make sure you mention the deadline and scarcity one more time.

Close the sale

If you were to have one of my webcasts transcribed, you'd hear me or my co-host say "click the order now button" or "visit www. MyProductDomain.com" to order the XYZ product right now at least a dozen times.

The more you connect and communicate taking immediate action and implementation with getting results, the more orders you get. When I started repeating the need to take action multiple times throughout the pitch portion of the webcast, our sales and orders increased by 20%-50%. Don't waste the opportunity to help more people and earn more income when you have an audience's attention!

As Zig Ziglar used to say, "Timid salesmen have skinny kids."

If your audience is still watching you and haven't purchased your product, it's because you haven't overcome an objection, injected a strong reason to buy, shared enough benefits, presented a strong enough guarantee, scarcity or deadline.

The art of the close is asking enough questions in chat to uncover whatever those "reasons" are - so stick around, ask more questions and earn the trust of your viewer!

Here are some keys to maximizing PROFIT.

Answer RELEVANT questions that support the sale. At any given time, 10% of your audience will likely be crazy people. They'll ask crazy questions that aren't relevant to your product or sale. Have someone on your team private message them in chat or in a worst case, ignore them or just kick them out of chat. If they're distraction or nuisance, it'll just get worse. Focus all of your energy on high-quality BUYERS, not the crazy, noisy time-wasters.

"Stay til the end…" The first item to add to any webcast is to make sure that at the very beginning and throughout, you announce to the audience that they need to stick around for the *entire* presentation because at the end they will be able to get a copy of your slides and have an opportunity to win a great prize. That way they stick around the entire time.

For example, you've read about our Apple Watch giveaway. We say, "Take lots of notes, because the question that we're going to ask a question we cover in presentation and the first person to type the correct answer in chat is going to be the lucky winner of the Apple Watch." Then during the entire show, we keep reminding the attendees that the Apple Watch giveaway is coming up and so is the link for the slides.

When we get to the close (the selling part of the show), we ask for permission, letting everyone know that the slide deck is coming up, the Apple Watch is coming up, and the Q&A is coming up.

Finally, after we go through the offer we say,"To get a copy of the slides, click the Order Now button below this video and at the bottom of the page is the link to download the slides and that link will disappear tonight at midnight."

You must make sure there is an offer deadline, which is a specific day and a specific time. Ideally, you've got a countdown timer on that sales page that is counting down for that time, for example Sunday at midnight.

Next thing that we do is say, "There's a countdown timer that's running right now, and we have some fast action bonuses for anyone who takes advantage of this offer before the counter runs out." In other words, as soon as this timer finishes counting down, these two bonuses are going to go away, so that way in our case we had a bonus with clear value. Make it clear to the audience, this special bonus goes away when the timer ends.

The Highest Value Fast Action Bonus: Next, we have another bonus and this is something it's got an incredibly high value proposition. It should be something valuable like some time with you (the star), extra training, or a complementary product. Often the extra bonus requires implementation on their part, meaning they have to complete the entire program, fill out a survey, and submit their questions in order to qualify for that bonus. This ensures your product gets used, implemented or consumed.

RESET!: When the timer runs out, you'll say, "I know we've been answering questions. Now we're going to do the Apple Watch giveaway.

GIVEAWAY: We ask a question, it's relevant to whatever the offer is. The first person who types in the correct answer to this question in chat is declared the winner, then thank them, reinforce and summarize the offer one more time and the urgency in taking action.

Then, you get to the end of the offer and the summary and do the final close.

The more you practice, the better you'll get at this and I genuinely believe it's the one of the most valuable (and profitable) skills and talents you'll ever learn.

WATCH A VIDEO CLOSE

It's much easier to SHOW you a close than describe it to you. Below is a link to a webcast that walks through a "proper close" and you can get a copy of my current slide presentation that you can model for your own webcasts.

You'll also receive the latest copy of this book in digital format with some other great gifts.

Register right now at www.WebcastProfitToolkit.com

Chapter 7: Resources - Join Me for a Free Webcast

Each chapter of this book includes a specific "call to action" for a free gift including a copy of my "How to Be a Video Interview Pro" book and a chance to watch a live or encore presentation of a profitable webcast.

The best ways to learn a new skill is to either observe and model what you want to learn, dive in and do it or get trained and coached by someone who's been doing it a long time.

I'd love for you to take the next step, register for my "Webcast Profit Toolkit" webcast and see how I present on video and show an offer that you can model for your business.

You'll also receive a copy of my slide presentation so you can see how I construct a profitable webcast and present an offer in a way that makes you and an audience feel good.

When you attend the webcast, make sure you introduce yourself in chat and let me know how you first learned about me!

I'm looking forward to getting to know you better and to hear your stories of profitable webcast success!

Sincerely,
Mike Koenigs
San Diego, CA

Chapter 8: More Success Stories

I try to capture as many endorsements and testimonials as I can from clients and customers. I play testimonial and case study videos during my webcasts to add credibility and connection with the audience.

People often feel they might not be able to be as good as you are at something – because you're so experienced, make things look easy and they feel like they're too far behind and can never catch up.

Playing "ordinary people" or "mess to success" transformational stories overcomes these objections, builds trust and connects you more deeply with your viewers.

· ·

Dr. Pillay

"My name is Dr. Srini Pillay. I'm a part-time assistant professor at Harvard Medical School, and the CEO of Neurobusiness Group. I'm here today to tell you one simple fact. Webcasting is the future of spreading messages. The reason I think this is that I think deep within every expert is this desire to spread a message worldwide.

When we think about spreading a message the old way, we've got to cave in to publishers. We've got to cave in to traditional media. You don't really have the ability to craft your own message the way you want it to be. The reason I'm here today and the reason I'm elated about the whole webcasting experience is that we were able to craft a message that we truly believed in a market that we actually understand intimately and differently from television executives.

For me, the experience of working with Mike Koenigs and JJ Virgin was really incredible from a number of different perspectives. I think first of all, having their expertise about the content and the way to reach people and being trained to do webcasting was really phenomenal. Secondly, Mike's energy is off the charts. I really think that if you ever want to webcast, you really need someone like him to walk you through the process.

My experience of working with Mike is an incredible opportunity, not just to work on and spread your own message, but to leverage the collective intelligence of people you truly love and respect so that you can get to the people who need your message now.

Webcasting is the way, and Mike is your way to get there."

. . . .

Diego Rodriguez

"My name is Diego Rodriguez. I'm the founder of the Power Marketing Consultants Network. I just want to tell you about how important video and webcasting has been to our business. We've generated over $1 million in sales using video and webcasting specifically in the last three years.

I didn't know anything about webcasting until I met Mike Koenigs. I learned about the production and business models from him. I'd obviously recommend that you take advantage of any opportunity to learn about webcasting from him. Not only do we use webcasting for our business, but we sell the service to our customers too.

You can use it for anything and everything. I honestly believe it's the way with the future. Anyone who doesn't get into webcasting is going to get left in the dust. Let me just give you a couple of real quick examples of how we use it for our clients.

One of my customers has a large national network of salespeople...

Instead of only connecting with all the salespeople once year at a national sales conference, we started a monthly webcast where we connect everyone, share best practices, do live training, and keep everyone updated. This has made a significant impact on their business and the culture of the company.

Another client I have is a contractor. He built the training program for other contractors that we sold online. We used Mike's webcasting model and sold over $204,000 in only eight days.

Let me share how we use webcasting and how you can use it too. You could use it for doctors and dentists to connect with their customers, for mortgage brokers to speak to realtors, for plumbers and electricians to teach home improvement.

I could go on and on and on. Here is the thing, brothers and sisters. webcasting is the future. If you're not doing it, you need to do it. We're doing it, and the results are incredible. I learned it all from Mike. I can't encourage you enough to learn about it from him too.

If you get a chance to learn how to webcast from Mike Koenigs, do it."

Programs and Products
by Mike Koenigs

Quickly and easily produce profitable webcasts, start your own online interactive TV show or infomercial channel, build a list, grow an audience, promote, market and sell your products, services or brand...even if you aren't a techie.

This is the ultimate video marketing training system for entrepreneurs, small business owners, authors, experts, speakers, coaches, consultants and creatives to share your message *powerfully and intimately*.

What is the "Webcast Profit Toolkit"?

Have you ever watched an infomercial on TV or online and wondered how they're made and how you could promote, market and sell your products, services or you in a highly interactive and educational way to make money without having to sell in person, on stage...at almost no risk or cost?

What if it was easy to do and took just a couple of hours to get started with equipment you already own and know how to use?

The Webcast Profit Toolkit is an online training course that teaches entrepreneurs, small business owners, authors, experts, speakers, coaches, consultants and creative types how to start their own Interactive Online Television Shows to sell or create products and services.

"Webcasts" are just like TV infomercials except they are interactive and can be produced and broadcast for free using equipment you already own and know how to use. The Webcast Profit Toolkit teaches you how to use low-cost computers and camera equipment and produce a compelling, educational, entertaining business show that gets viewers interested in any product or service.

Visit www.WebcastToolkit.com for a free training webcast and more information.

Book Mike to Speak!

Book Mike Koenigs as your Keynote Speaker and You're Guaranteed to Make Your Event Highly Entertaining and Unforgettable!

For over two decades, 9-time #1 bestselling author, serial entrepreneur, angel investor and philanthropist, Mike Koenigs has been educating, entertaining and helping entrepreneurs, authors, experts, speakers, consultants and coaches build and grow their businesses with the online video, social media, mobile and product creation strategies.

His origin story includes his recent near-death brush with stage 3a cancer, growing up lower middle-class in a small town in Eagle Lake Minnesota, severe ADHD and "meeting" Tony Robbins through an infomercial that changed his life forever. After successfully building and exiting from two companies and selling them to publicly-traded companies, Mike can share relevant, actionable strategies that anyone can use - even if they're starting from scratch.

His unique style inspires, empowers and entertains audiences while giving them the tools and strategies they need and want to get seen, heard, build and grow successful sustainable brands and businesses.

Speaking topics include:

- **Publish and Profit:** How to Write, Publish, Promote and Become a #1 Bestselling Author in Less than 30 Days

- **How to Save the World with Video:** Five Key Things Every Video Needs to Connect with an Audience

- **Defying Death – The Cancerpreneur:** How You, Your Marriage, Relationship with Your Children, Friendships, Clients and Business Can Survive a Cancer Diagnosis and Treatment

- **You Everywhere Now!** How to Be Seen, Heard, Viewed, Listened to Anywhere, Anytime on Any Device and Build an Intimate Relationship with an Engaged Audience

- **The Big Lever:** Discover Your Manifestation Machine, Model the Wisdom and Experience of the Hyper-Successful to Crank Up Your Credibility, Productivity and Impact

- **$1,000,000 in 100 Day Blueprint:** 7 Commandments to Producing Twelve Consecutive Multimillion Dollar Product Launches

- **Product Creation Master Plan:** How to Turn Any Idea into a Profitable Product in 30 Days in Any Market

- **Star Power!** How to Launch an Online TV Show or Podcast, Interview Like a Pro and Be Comfortable and Compelling on Camera

- **Your Superpowers and Fatal Flaws:** How to Be More Creative, Charismatic, Productive and Operate in the "Zone"

- **Distruptasaurus!** How to Disrupt a Market, Go Viral and Build a World-Class Brand

- **Built to Sell:** How To Build and Sell a Successful Business

For more info, visit www.MikeKoenigs.com/speaking or call +1 (858) 412-0858.

Made in the USA
Monee, IL
29 May 2021